WHEN DIFFICULT RELATIVES HAPPEN TO GOOD PEOPLE

WHEN DIFFICULT RELATIVES HAPPEN TO GOOD PEOPLE

SURVIVING YOUR FAMILY
AND KEEPING YOUR SANITY

LEONARD FELDER, PH.D.

RODALE

Notice

This book is intended as a reference volume only, not as a medical manual. The information given here is designed to help you make informed decisions about your health. It is not intended as a substitute for any treatment that may have been prescribed by your doctor. If you suspect that you have a medical problem, we urge you to seek competent medical help. Also, reading about family conflicts can be stressful for some people. If you have been diagnosed with a serious mental illness, or if you have ever been prescribed medication for a psychiatric condition, or if you are feeling agitated while thinking about this topic, it is recommended that you consult with a qualified physician or mental health professional before reading or utilizing any of the suggestions in this book.

The names and identifying details in the case histories in this book have been changed to protect confidentiality.

Printed in the United States of America
Rodale Inc. makes every effort to use acid-free (∞), recycled paper ♻.

Book design by Joanna Williams

Library of Congress Cataloging-in-Publication Data

Felder, Leonard.
    When difficult relatives happen to good people : surviving your family and keeping your sanity / Leonard Felder.
        p.   cm.
    ISBN 1-57954-763-X hardcover
    1. Family—Psychological aspects.   2. Interpersonal conflict.   3. Conflict management.   I. Title.
    HQ734.F373   2003
    306.85—dc21   2003013939

Distributed to the book trade by St. Martin's Press
2   4   6   8   10   9   7   5   3   1   hardcover

Visit us on the Web at www.rodalestore.com, or call us toll-free at (800) 848-4735.

RODALE

WE **INSPIRE** AND **ENABLE** PEOPLE TO IMPROVE
THEIR LIVES AND THE WORLD AROUND THEM

To my amazing sister, Janice.

Even though we are different from each other,

the love and closeness will last forever.

ACKNOWLEDGMENTS

This book has been blessed with the contributions of many caring and supportive people. My agent Andrew Stuart guided it wisely from the start. The staff at Rodale has been helpful in so many ways: Stephanie Tade, Amy Rhodes, Troy Juliar, Chris Potash, Cathy Gruhn, Mary Lengle, Dana Bacher, Leslie Schneider, Kelly Schmidt, Jackie Dornblaser, and numerous others worked hard to make this project a success.

Additional insights and help were offered by good friends Teri Bernstein, Peter and Carol Reiss, Marc Sirinsky and Catherine Coulson, Trudi Alexy, Deborah Bronner, Sandra Kaler, Laura Pawlowski, Miriam Raviv, Beth Rosenberg, Harriet Shapiro, Anita Siegman, and Barbara Zheutlin. I am also grateful to the men and women who taught me over the years to write and do psychological research—James Michael, Sean Austin, and Rowland Shepard at Kenyon College, Tom Bonoma at the University of Pittsburgh, Harold Bloomfield and Adelaide Bry in San Diego.

Several members of my own family have been enormously loving and supportive to my work. They include Martin and Ena Felder, Helen Rothenberg Felder, Janice, Craig, and Erica Ruff, Nellie Kolb, Andi Bittker, Ruthe McCabe, Ron Wagner, the Schorin and Wilstein families in Pitts-

burgh and Los Angeles, the Bayer family in New York and
Vermont, and the Felder and Rothenberg families in Michigan
and Florida.

I especially want to thank my creative and loving wife
and best friend Linda Schorin, as well as our wonderful son
Steven, for all the warmth and joy they bring to each day.
And I thank God that I have been given the chance to work
as a therapist and a writer on a topic as compelling as this.

CONTENTS

INTRODUCTION

Why do difficult relatives happen to good people? I've found that no matter how smart or nice you are, there is still a high likelihood that at least one member of your immediate or extended family will hurt you or someone you love. Just flash back on the incidents in recent months and years when a parent, stepparent, in-law, ex-spouse, aunt, uncle, sister, brother, son, daughter, or other family member did or said something that made you want to explode.

Now imagine for a moment what your life would be like if you could avoid getting stressed or upset when interacting with these crazy-making relatives. What kind of vitality and energy would be freed up if you spent less time arguing and strategizing inside your own head about how—or if—to deal with your difficult relatives? How would it feel if you knew your next family gathering wasn't going to be dominated or ruined by a certain individual because you could handle the situation? *When Difficult Relatives Happen to Good People* will show you how.

A WIDESPREAD PROBLEM

It's been a number of years since I coauthored the best-selling book *Making Peace with Your Parents* and began giving workshops throughout the country on making peace within your family. Wherever I go, I'm always amazed at the number and variety of decent people who take me aside to tell me their private stories of dealing with difficult relatives.

Based on a nationwide research study I've been conducting, I've found that a majority of Americans experience significant tension at one or more family events each year, especially at Thanksgiving, Christmas, Hanukah, Passover, Easter, weddings, birthdays, funerals, and other rites of passage. Even if there is a geographical buffer between you and your relatives, there is likely to be an underlying discomfort every time you speak on the telephone or inevitably find yourself at a family function face to face with a particular sibling, parent, in-law, grown child, or other problem relative.

In terms of actual numbers, I've interviewed a random sample of 1,358 men and women from a range of races, ethnicities, income groups, and family configurations. I had expected that maybe 30 to 40 percent of Americans would describe their family gatherings as tense or difficult. But to my surprise, I found that 75 percent of men and women have at least one family member who gets on their nerves, and 68 percent of us describe family celebrations as either frustrating or an obligation that we don't enjoy. (For the complete results of my polling research, please see the appendix on page 287.)

It's clear from this study that there are more people who experience stress than bliss with their extended families. No matter how many magazines you read about setting a lovely table or preparing the perfect meal, the problem still remains: How do you keep difficult relatives from ruining your chance to celebrate life with the irreplaceable people in your extended family who won't be around forever?

"I DON'T KNOW HOW I'M GONNA SURVIVE MY HUSBAND'S FAMILY"

Each of us has a unique family, and yet there are certain personality types and typical conflicts that show up in millions of American families. Do any of the following sound familiar?

> Elaine has a very opinionated mother-in-law. In fact, I remember one session in which Elaine told me her mother-in-law was keeping a notebook of the things Elaine was doing wrong. "My husband saw the notebook sitting on my mother-in-law's kitchen table. It was filled with things she doesn't like about how I dress, how I don't keep the house clean enough, and how I'm not doing things right for her son and her grandchildren. I don't know how I'm gonna survive my husband's family."

> Bruce is a terrific high school teacher who has won awards for his creative programs helping inner-city kids become successful in life. The one time when Bruce feels like a failure, however, is when he visits his family. "My dad is a lawyer, my brother is a

lawyer, and my sister is an investment banker. When I show up at family dinners, they glance at my ten-year-old car and they give me a look that says, 'Poor Bruce, he's such a loser.' I sometimes wonder why I keep showing up for these family torture sessions."

Krista is possibly the most amazing event planner you'll ever meet. She can arrange enormously interesting dinner parties and create spectacular celebrations for her friends' birthdays. The only Krista-arranged events that are likely to bomb are when she has her relatives over for a family holiday. "There just doesn't seem to be a way to bring my relatives together without it turning into a painful mess. My father and his new wife both drink too much and start saying things that suck the air out of the room. My twenty-two-year-old daughter loves to stir up trouble; last year at the holidays, she showed up with a new boyfriend who could only be described as on hiatus between prison stays. My older brother the doctor is married to an incredible snob who always finds something about me to criticize. I've also got two cousins who can't be seated at the same table because they had a falling out in business with each other and the bitterness flares up whenever they're together. Next year I think we should all go to McDonald's and order the Happy Meals."

If you're being honest, chances are you can relate to at least one of these situations, or to a similar story involving your own family but with its own, maddening twist.

WHAT CAN BE DONE?

If there's someone in your family that you don't get along with—or, perhaps they don't get along with you—then do something about it. For instance, if there is a specific family member whose sole purpose in living seems to be to push your buttons, let's find a way to reduce the impact this person has on you. Or if there is a family event that you dread attending because you know there's going to be tension, let's work on a way to make this event less stressful and more fulfilling. Or if you find yourself trying so hard to juggle the needs of *all* your difficult relatives that you're at your wit's end, let's remedy the situation.

In this book, you will find easy-to-follow, practical steps you can take in order to:

- Understand more deeply what causes the tensions in your particular family.
- Sort out which relatives you can get closer to and which ones to keep at a distance.

- Identify what makes phone calls and visits so problematic, and what you can do to help improve these basic family interactions.

- Clarify and come to terms with the money, status, and competition issues that are causing friction between members of your family.

- Explore and offer creative solutions for the religious disagreements and lifestyle/values clashes that are flaring up in more families today than ever before.

- Find out why people in your family tend to make hurtful or insensitive comments about each other's weight, appearance, or other touchy subjects—and what you can do to keep family events from turning into a dreadful onslaught of criticism and advice-giving.

- Learn what you can control and what you can't control regarding family members who have addictions to drugs, alcohol, gambling, and other problems.

- Heal your own heart from past hurts and disappointments with your family, so that you can make sure you break the multigenerational legacies of pain that can do damage to your own children and your adult romantic partner.

- Learn profound lessons about your own life's journey and personal growth by examining what you want to keep and what you want to discard from your family patterns.

- Find the right words to confront family members who are abusive or hurtful, and avoid approaches that might make matters worse.

When Difficult Relatives Happen to Good People uses humor, true stories, and helpful insights to address one of life's most perplexing challenges: how to get along better with even your most difficult relative.

WHAT TO EXPECT

I can't promise that if you read this book your self-centered sister will miraculously become a compassionate human being, or that your wealthy, belligerent uncle will learn humility. But I will predict that if you think about and utilize some of the suggestions I offer, you can become far more skilled at surviving your time with them with your sanity intact.

In addition to the stories and techniques that come from counseling my clients and workshop participants, I will include a few examples from my own family. Both my wife, Linda, and I have several relatives whom we love in our hearts but are quite frankly challenging to deal with.

I remember one particular holiday dinner when a few aunts and uncles were screaming at each other in a huge argument. These adult siblings who love one another were nevertheless ripping into each other verbally and saying extremely hurtful things. I turned to Linda's ninety-year-old grandmother to see if the shouting match was upsetting her. Grandma Ruth, who had a great sense of humor, looked around and then looked back at me as she said calmly, "Isn't it great to have the family together again?"

Another time, my wife and I were driving home from an especially stressful family event. We were exhausted from all the tension of the evening. There was a long silence in the car. Then, out of nowhere, Linda said in an ironic tone of voice, "It's all relatives." We both started laughing.

I mention these two stories because I want you to know how important humor, a sense of irony, and a positive perspective can be in dealing with even extremely serious and painful family issues.

One of the key themes of this book is that even if you can't change your relatives, you can significantly change and improve how you respond to them. In each of the chapters that follows, you will learn how to stop falling into the same traps and battles that have frustrated you in the past. You will discover creative ways to transform your family get-togethers, even if your difficult relative continues to exhibit the same personality traits that used to ruin each interaction. In addition, this book will give you personal insight that can help you feel a lot less victimized and a lot more comfortable with your family.

I strongly believe, and have seen repeatedly, that our family interactions are like a crucible where we get tested and shaped by heated emotions and fiery disputes. In a meaningful way, your family difficulties will force you to figure out who you really are—or else your relatives will dictate who they expect you to be.

Over the years I've counseled many terrific people who've felt that their psyches and souls were being trampled by certain relatives. My hope is that this book will help you or someone you love find solid ways to be protected against such hurt. I also will be suggesting numerous ways in which your spirit may become stronger and more alive as a result of these encounters with your relatives. My intention is that this book will not only improve the quality of your family gatherings, but also transform the way you feel inside when you are face to face with your most difficult relatives.

WHEN
DIFFICULT
RELATIVES
HAPPEN
TO GOOD
PEOPLE

CHAPTER ONE

WHY DO CERTAIN RELATIVES UPSET YOU AT SUCH A DEEP LEVEL?

L et's face it—there are times when family members do hurtful, selfish, insensitive, obnoxious things. It might be a father or father-in-law who can't stop offering unsolicited advice and criticism, or a mother or mother-in-law who tries to make you feel guilty for having a life of your own. It could be a stepparent or stepchild who feels threatened by you and does things to make your life miserable. It might be a sister or brother who receives preferential treatment, or who has never stopped trying to one-up you. Maybe it's a grown daughter or son—or grandchild—who frustrates you with his or her unreliability. It might be a member of the family who is terribly judgmental about your personal life, or one who tries to shove religious or political beliefs down your throat.

As a psychologist, the first thing I do is check with the person sitting in front of me to gauge if the family issue bothering him or her feels like a tiny irritation or a significant upset. Does the relative strongly get on your nerves or is the

3

person easy to ignore? It would be wrong for a therapist to rush into an assumption that some family incident has deep meaning when it doesn't. Despite what Freud may have said a hundred years ago, sometimes a cigar is just a cigar—and sometimes a complaint about an obnoxious family member is just a minor speed bump on the highway of life.

But for most of us there are, from time to time, hurtful family interactions that hit us especially hard and need to be addressed. There are certain confrontations that stick in your psyche and undermine your sense of well-being with surprising ferocity. You may have said to yourself, "Oh, I'm just going to ignore so-and-so. He's done this crap before and he'll probably do it again." But something in your head or your gut just won't let it go this time. Something about this person's insensitivity is gnawing at your insides and you will need to discover what it is so you can regain your peace of mind and your optimum effectiveness.

Think back on your recent family get-togethers. Are there some family members who can spout off and act less than civil toward you and you can shrug it off or ignore it, while other relatives get under your skin and make you want to scream for the least little comment? Who are these relatives that make you want to lash out in anger? What are the incidents that still make your blood boil when you think about them? It's important to identify who's who, because if you try to gloss over your strong emotional upset regarding certain relatives you will only make matters worse. Pretending you are fine when you are actually seething inside only causes the unexplored hurt feelings to grab hold of your psyche even stronger.

Based on what I've learned from my clients and workshop participants over the past twenty years, there are two basic ways of understanding why certain relatives and certain incidents upset you on a deep level. As you think about the frustrations you have in your own family, ask yourself which of the following explanations rings most true for you

YOU MIGHT BE EMBARRASSED

When your own flesh and blood says or does something offensive or cruel, it's got to make you wonder, "Am I really related to this person? How can that be?" For example, you may be shocked when your own brother insults a guest you've brought to dinner. Or you might feel the sting of resentment when your spoiled cousin or opinionated aunt comments that you'd look great if only you'd lose ten pounds. Or maybe you're humiliated when your child acts up in public and you feel the glare of onlookers as they say under their breath, "Doesn't that parent know how to control her kid?" Or you might be mortified when your parents or in-laws say the tackiest things in front of someone you had hoped to impress.

I've found that a common reason people get angry and hurt by the obnoxious behavior of their family members is because they believe that the misbehavior or abrasive personality of their relative is a direct reflection on them. Particularly if you are a caring and sensitive person, you might think, "I'm not safe being seen in public with this relative," or "I'll never be able to show my face again if people know I'm related to this person who's so inappropriate." It may feel as if your most obnoxious relative is announcing to the world, "This is who we really are! We have absolutely no class and don't let anyone fool you into thinking otherwise!" It's like you are holding your breath, hoping no one will notice that you come from the same gene pool.

Relatives Are Strange by Design

If you stop for a moment and look at the situation from a scientific perspective, it makes perfect sense that you are not responsible and should not feel embarrassed about the sometimes-strange behavior that goes on in your family. In fact, from a scientific perspective it is clear that in every family there tends to be at least one individual who is troubled, unpleasant, insensitive, or worse.

In the past ten years there have been some exciting discoveries by the scientists conducting the human genome project in which our personality traits and other genetic predispositions are being mapped according to the chromosomes, enzymes, and biochemical variations that strongly influence how we look and act. One of the remarkable findings has been that there seems to be, *by design*, a range and severity of personality diversity among members of the same family. Par-

ents who have more than one child know this to be true—
from early infancy each kid has a distinct and unique personality. Just because relatives may be alike in many of their
physical and other features, their personalities can still be
quite different.

What's especially revealing in the human genome research is that *within every family there tends to be a full range
of individual variations on a particular personality trait.* Let's
take for instance a personality factor such as self-absorbed behavior. You know what a narcissist is: In the Greek myth,
Narcissus only wanted to look at his own reflection. It's the
member of your family who loves talking about himself, who
thinks the world revolves around her. It's the person in your
family who feels entitled to special treatment or who always
wants things her own way. It's the family member who might
do something nice for you but only if it flatters his self-image
in the long run.

Genetic research shows that in families there are usually
one or two people who are prone to narcissistic tendencies.
These "huge dose" individuals tend to be charming but arrogant, driven, inflexible, and unable to have empathy for the
needs and feelings of others.

In this same family you might have one or two others
who were born with a medium dose of the biochemistry that
favors narcissism. These "medium dose" individuals have
selfish moments but can be empathic at times. They are ambitious but capable of considering the needs and feelings of

others as well. They have far less self-absorption than the flaming narcissists in the family, but enough drive and self-worth to be successful in the world.

Finally, in this same family there often is a third type of person who received a significantly lower dose of the genes, chromosomes, and enzymes that lead to narcissism. This third type of family member might have a painfully low level of self-centeredness and a huge helping of empathy and flexibility. This extra-nice individual sometimes gets treated like a sounding board or even at times a doormat by the more narcissistic members of the family.

In most families, people tend to judge and criticize one another for exhibiting different levels of a particular personality trait. The highly self-absorbed/narcissistic family member might be thinking or saying, "I wish my other family members weren't such whiny pushovers and losers." At the same time, the less narcissistic family members might be thinking or saying, "I wish my other family members weren't so obnoxiously self-centered and demanding." In most cases, the various family members feel upset and offended at the idea that someone from their own family is so different from what he or she thinks is the right way to be. Rather than accepting that each family is genetically designed to exhibit a diversity of personality traits, we spend a lot of time and energy feeling horrified, hurt, or angry that our relatives are so unlike us.

What if you were to embrace the diversity in your family

and say to yourself, "What an amazing collection of different characters we are. What an odd combination of seemingly incompatible personalities we were born with in this family. Bring it on!" What if instead of resisting the mysterious spiritual and biological design of the universe, you could simply take a deep, relaxing breath and say, "Wow, we've got an empathic caregiver and a self-absorbed bully in the same family gene pool!"

I'm not saying you have to bury your head in the sand and give up completely on trying to help or influence your loved ones. If a member of your family is looking to change and asks you for assistance, you should feel free to help him in whatever way you can. If an impulsive or insensitive family member needs someone to set a firm limit for her so that she won't trample on the feelings and needs of others, then by all means do. And, if a family member's hurtful habits or mental illness are severe enough, try your best to be a positive influence. Point him in the direction of a good therapist, an appropriate medication, or an inspiring coach or mentor, but don't feel responsible for his inappropriate behavior. As Reinhold Niebuhr said so eloquently almost eighty years ago, "Please grant me the serenity to accept the things I cannot change, to change those things I can change, and to recognize the difference." (See Chapters Two and Three for more on setting healthy limits with difficult relatives.)

One of the best ways to break free of the pain of having a difficult relative is to remind yourself—often!—not to feel guilty, shocked, or offended by what is beyond your control. Even though you may be related to this person, you are not able to control his thoughts, actions, or words. Or at least I hope you don't have that job—it would be so time-consuming and exhausting to try to run someone else's life.

Using Humor to Unhook from Your Usual Reaction

What can you do during a tense moment to break the habit of becoming upset, enraged, or embarrassed because of the misbehavior of a difficult relative? The next time you are in a public place with a parent, child, in-law, or other relative who does something that normally would make you want to cringe or explode, try saying to yourself, with ironic humor, "I'll bet everyone in sight is thinking I am somehow related to this person. Hah! What they don't know is that I have never ever met this person and I have no clue whatsoever as to why anyone would think otherwise." Or you can take some of the sting out of the situation by saying calmly to yourself, "I wonder whose relative that person is?" and just smile inside for a moment. Or you can say to yourself, "If I were somehow in control of my relative's personality or behavior, I definitely could feel upset right now. But since I'm not in charge of her life, I can just watch her with the detachment of an anthropologist from Sweden who would find this person fascinating, a bit bizarre, and most worthy of an entire dissertation."

This technique might not work every time, and there

still may be incidents that absolutely get under your skin. But if you practice detaching yourself, or your emotional well-being, from the other person's behavior, you will gradually see some progress. You are likely to find that you become much less bent out of shape by even your most difficult relative's nonsense. You will find that you can save yourself a lot of aggravation by looking at your family member with a compassionate calmness as you say, "We are different people—always have been and always will be."

"I Wonder Whose Daughter That Unpleasant Girl Might Be?"

To illustrate the practicality of dry humor and detachment, consider my client Bernice, who is a phenomenal parent (most of the time) but who happens to have an extremely volatile and oppositional teenage daughter named Jenna, who pushes Bernice beyond her limit every so often. After numerous incidents where Jenna's verbal insults and stubbornness caused Bernice to question why she ever became a parent, Bernice came in for counseling.

She told me, "I feel like I'm a complete failure with my daughter. Sometimes Jenna gets me so upset I start yelling back at her and I become almost as out of control as she is. I feel as though Jenna is determined to humiliate me in public, and I can't seem to separate the fact that she's a hormonal teenager and I'm supposed to be the sensible adult."

To help Bernice regain her inner strength and her ability

to be effective with a troubled teenager who needs an extremely resourceful, firm, and loving parent, I urged Bernice to try the detachment technique described above. We practiced a few comeback lines, and Bernice was ready the next time Jenna pushed her close to the edge.

A grand opportunity to try out the new technique occurred in a shopping mall a few days later. Jenna and Bernice were looking for a new outfit Jenna could wear to an important party that was coming up in two weeks. The search for the right dress was going well until Jenna pulled one of her usual stunts—trying to humiliate her mom in public. Jenna walked up to a stylishly dressed middle-aged sales clerk and said, within Bernice's earshot, "Can I tell you that you look great in that outfit? My mom would look awful if she tried to dress like that, but you look incredible."

Bernice calmly took a breath and said silently to herself, "I wonder whose daughter that unpleasant girl might be?" With a sense of inner strength she hadn't felt in a long time, Bernice knew at that moment she had begun to unhook from her old habit of taking it personally and getting out-of-control upset as a result of Jenna's provocative comments.

Bernice then said calmly to her daughter, "I'm so sorry our shopping trip has ended for today. We'll have another chance next week."

Jenna replied, "Ohmigod, Mother, I did not do anything."

Bernice still felt calm and in control as she said lovingly

but firmly, "I'm your mom and I'm in charge of making sure you don't say hurtful things to people you care about. So let's go and we'll try again next week because I *do* want to get you the outfit we talked about."

Jenna snapped back, "No way. We're gonna get the outfit now!"

Bernice calmly repeated to herself the humor line we had practiced, "I wonder whose daughter that unpleasant girl might be?" Then she firmly but softly whispered to Jenna, "If you make a scene or if you don't leave right now, we won't be going shopping next week either. It's your choice, Jenna, and for your sake I hope you make the right choice."

Jenna was stunned. Her mom had never been so calm and so resolved when taking away a privilege. Knowing that Bernice was fully in charge, Jenna silently followed her out of the store and back into the car. Like hundreds of other clients who have tried these techniques, Bernice had used silent humor and calm detachment to regain her power and clarity with a highly demanding family member.

"I Don't Know if We've Met That Unusual Older Gentleman"

Brian and Katrina used a similar but much less confrontational humor/detachment technique with Brian's divorced father, whose name is Walter. For years Brian and Katrina had felt humiliated and resentful at Walter's rudeness and pushiness in public places, especially when they took him to restaurants, where Walter usually felt compelled to boss around the hired help. Walter is an intense, self-made entrepreneur who always feels like he has to be in control. As he himself put it, "You either have to let people know who's boss or they'll walk all over you."

Brian and Katrina had made plans to take Walter out to a nice restaurant for his birthday, but they were worried that this dinner would be like dozens of others that had gone badly. Their concerns proved to be well founded, when as soon as they got to the restaurant Walter started bossing around the car valet, the restaurant manager, and the wine steward. He also kept sending the waiters and the busboy back for all sorts of things throughout the meal.

Brian recalled, "In the past, this birthday dinner would have been a disaster. I would have shut down emotionally with knots in my stomach. Katrina would have been upset because she would feel unable to let the hired help know that we don't agree with my dad's disrespectful way of treating people. We both would have felt victimized and humiliated, which is an extra price we pay on top of the huge credit card bill we would be signing to treat my dear old dad on his birthday."

But this year was different. Brian and Katrina had participated a few weeks earlier in a workshop I'd given on dealing with difficult relatives where they had learned the humor/detachment technique. Their goal was not to get into a power struggle with Walter or attempt to change his underlying personality. Rather, their intention was simply to get through the birthday dinner without feeling humiliated. And, possibly, to enjoy some quality moments of connecting with Brian's father, despite his imperfections.

Katrina explained, "When my father-in-law started doing his usual number on the restaurant staff, I whispered calmly to Brian, 'I don't know if we've met this unusual older gentleman.' It snapped both of us out of feeling tense or embarrassed. For the first time in years we each felt calm and in charge, even though Walter was doing what used to drive us up a wall. Brian made sure to give an extra-large tip and a personal apology to each of the mistreated employees. Since I wasn't preoccupied with judging or trying to change my father-in-law, I actually enjoyed Walter's stories and his colorful personality. Knowing that he wasn't going to be able to embarrass us this time helped us dodge the uncomfortable moments and focus instead on the fact that he can also be a loving, affectionate, and complicated human being."

Again, the goal is not to change your family member's personality, which in most cases you are powerless to do. But if you significantly change your own reaction to this person, you will find it much easier to notice his good qualities and not just focus on his difficult traits. You will be able to spend time with your most difficult family member and come away feeling a positive connection, even if he's his same old infuriating self.

There's a Yiddish expression that says, "If you're waiting for your relatives to change . . . you should live so long." My suggestion is that instead of holding your breath and saying, "I won't be happy until this person changes," you can be much more effective if you focus instead on how to remain healthy yourself. Using humor and detachment helps you regain your sense of maturity and calmness, which are crucial tools for getting through any family gathering successfully.

YOU MIGHT SEE A HIDDEN PART OF YOURSELF

Sometimes the reason we get so upset with our relatives is because we know deep inside that we might be, or we might have been at one time, a little bit like they are. For example, one of your relatives might be a problem drinker or cigarette smoker and you might be a passionate ex-drinker or ex-smoker who can't tolerate being around someone who reminds you of how you once were. Or one of your relatives might be extremely frugal with money—some would say cheap—and you don't like the part of yourself that is or once was extremely frugal with money.

Or if one of your relatives has a weight problem and you have spent a lot of time and energy trying to hide or overcome your own weight problem, you might feel angry or humiliated when your overweight relative reaches for that extra piece of dessert. Or if you are insecure about your own educational level or social status, then a relative's grammatical errors might make you cringe. Or if a family member has questionable taste in clothes, furnishings, or films and you don't want anyone to notice the fact that you also grew up on the less affluent side of town, then you might notice yourself feeling horrified every time your family member commits a fashion faux pas.

As a psychotherapist, I find it fascinating and useful whenever I hear a counseling client getting upset or ranting about a family member's imperfections. It is usually the beginning of a wonderful opportunity for growth for the person sitting in front of me. Specifically, if you take a step back and look at each of the times you feel embarrassed or horrified by someone in your family, you may be able to identify the personal issues that make you most self-conscious, self-critical, or insecure.

In this way, your family member's disturbing behavior provides you with a valuable road map of issues you will need to face yourself if you are going to become a more healthy, relaxed, and self-accepting person. In fact, making a mental note of the things you can't stand about your relatives gives you a crucial set of clues as to what you may want to improve in yourself.

The "Thank You for Being So Unpleasant" Card

I sometimes advise my counseling clients to write *but not send* an unusual thank-you note to their most obnoxious or insensitive family member, saying something like, "Dear _____, I am so glad you are in my life. Because of you, I have seen more clearly than ever how I don't want to treat people. You are a brilliant example of exactly what I don't want to be like. Thank you for being an example that I will carry inside my mind and utilize for the rest of my life."

Some clients have enjoyed simply speaking these words aloud in my office, while others have actually written out the "Thank you for being so unpleasant" card. Whether you say these words to a counselor or friend, or whether you write them down and then tear up the card, the goal is to help you tap your sense of humor and your sense of clarity about how this difficult relative is an "inspiration"—of exactly the kind of person you don't want to become. I insist that you *do not* send the card to your relative because that would surely stir up additional friction and feuds.

There is an important second step in this technique of learning about the type of person you would like to be. The second step is to write down on a piece of paper the two divergent sets of qualities you see in this difficult family member who has been getting on your nerves. Answer the following questions, perhaps in a journal:

1. What traits of this relative do I admire and want to emulate?

2. What traits of this relative do I despise and want to avoid in my own life?

3. What kind of changes should I make and what help will I need to ensure that I don't perpetuate in my

own life what I have found so offensive in this family member?

Instead of just getting upset at your difficult relatives, this powerful exercise allows you to learn about yourself and become wiser and healthier. It's as though your most frustrating family members hold a secret gift for you—some clues about the struggle to become a far more compassionate, creative, and decent person than he or she has been.

"She's Just a Ditz"

To illustrate this exercise, I'll use the example of a client named Carol, a divorced woman in her thirties who entered therapy because she wanted to find out what was holding her back from having a successful love relationship. If you met Carol, you'd be shocked to find out that she has been without a serious romantic partner for almost nine years. She's attractive, intelligent, and extremely considerate to her parents, her friends from work, and her elderly neighbors in the apartment building where she lives.

But when I ask Carol about her family background, I see her face turn a bit red with anger as she begins to describe her painful estrangement from her younger sister, Patricia, who has been married three times. "We were very close when we were young kids, but I have been upset with Patricia for many years. She's just a ditz—I'd say she has as much common sense as a gerbil."

I learn that Carol is angry with her younger sister because Patricia "always throws herself at men. She's caused my parents huge amounts of heartache. And she continues to be extremely unreliable and immature. Every time there's a family gathering and Patricia shows up, late as usual, I feel like taking her aside and screaming at her to grow up already."

In this counseling session with Carol, I have two choices. I can just nod my head in agreement and not ask her to go too deeply into her own issues. Or I can begin to help Carol do some inner work and turn her frustrations about her younger sister into an opportunity for growth.

As you can probably guess, I choose to go for the inner work. I ask Carol, "Would you be interested in finding out whether your strong negative feelings about Patricia might be a clue about some important issues that are stirring inside of you?"

Carol is a little unsure at first. She says, "What do you mean? I'm just telling you why I can't stand my sister. This has nothing to do with me or my issues."

I ask Carol to trust me for a moment, and I promise that if the exercise I suggested feels uncomfortable or uninformative, we can move on to something else. She agrees to give it a try, so I give her a pad of paper and ask her to write down her first reactions to these three questions:

1. Is there anything about Patricia that you do like and would want to incorporate into your own life?

2. Is it possible that Patricia's behavior is upsetting because it reminds you of something that is hidden or unexpressed in your own personality?

3. Is there anything about Patricia that you would be willing to describe in an unusual thank-you note (and not send) to say how much you have learned from Patricia about the kind of person you do not want to be?

This brings a smile to Carol's face. She quickly writes a scathing thank-you note:

Dear Patricia,

Thank you for being such a perfect example of the kind of woman I don't want to be. You dress like a fancy hooker and you let men treat you like dirt. You make terrible decisions, always in a rush, without thinking through the consequences. You are the high priestess of self-sabotage. Keeping you in mind will help me make sure I don't fall into the traps you've repeatedly fallen into.

Then we discuss Patricia's good qualities—her spontaneity, her love of music and dance, her joie de vivre, and her love of animals, especially how well she cares for her three cats and two dogs.

Finally, we consider the first question. For a moment, Carol is silent. Then a tear begins to emerge from one of her eyes and slowly move down across her cheek.

Carol takes a minute more to let her thoughts wander and then tells me, "When I was in high school I was a lot like Patricia. I was fun, creative, full of life. But I got pregnant by accident and after a long, painful process of trying to make the right decision, I got an abortion. And the guy took off. Ever since then I've been extremely cautious and guarded in relationships, which is understandable, I guess. But I've also been very resentful of Patricia and her wild life. It's upsetting just to be around her and see her doing things in such a carefree way. I don't understand it, but I get quite agitated inside just from hearing her stories or seeing how she acts."

Over the next several sessions, Carol and I work to sort through these complex issues and emotions. We do some intensive grief work to explore her feelings regarding the abortion and about being betrayed by the boyfriend. I direct Carol to write a series of thank-you notes to Patricia (that were torn up and never sent) in which Carol pours out her feelings about how much she has learned from witnessing Patricia's mistakes with men.

We also begin to explore the aspects of Carol and Patricia's "wildness" that are acceptable or unacceptable to Carol now. Knowing all that she knows and having experienced all that she has experienced, Carol is able to sort out calmly what kind of cautiousness she feels is necessary and what kind of sensuality she now is willing to explore.

This inner work, which was first triggered by Carol's strongly judgmental feelings about her younger sister, became the basis for several breakthroughs in Carol's life. Carol gradually opened up a bit in her relationships with men and began dating more regularly. She also became a lot less judgmental of Patricia, and much closer to her. As Carol explained, "Patricia is still not the sharpest blade on the saw when it comes to her dealings with men. But I don't feel as agitated about her private business as I once did. Now when Patricia and I get together for dinner and a movie, or a visit to a museum, we don't try to change each other. We just enjoy being sisters again with a whole lot of closeness and warmth. She still is a bit of a ditz. But she's family and she's taught me a heck of a lot about how to put on makeup, how to change my haircut to bring out my best features, and how to accessorize my favorite outfits. We sometimes disagree about things, and we occasionally argue, but we both know that our love for each other is deeper than whatever tensions flare up between us. After years of being enemies, we're just plain old sisters again, and I'm glad she's in my life."

Carol recently met a man and it looks promising that their relationship may lead to marriage and a family. She's been fortunate that the man she's fallen in love with is quite self-aware and willing to do the hard work of making a relationship successful. He's caring enough to know that Carol has been betrayed before and needs to be treated with a great deal of honesty and respect.

I can't guarantee that everyone who writes an unsent note saying "Thank you for being such a horrific example of who I don't want to be" is going to have a reconciliation with his family member or a breakthrough in her personal life. But I do promise that you will gain a lot of wisdom about who you are and what you want to become if you stop judging your family members and start using their imperfections as a clue for your own inner searching.

Why not start today? Whenever you notice yourself getting worked up or self-righteous about the misbehavior of someone in your family, be sure to slow down and ask yourself: What positive traits do I want to pick up from this person? What hidden or unexpressed aspect of my own personality is this person forcing me to look at? What negative traits do I want to avoid?

If you utilize this technique, you are bound to find yourself reacting a lot less when your relatives misbehave. Instead, you will be able to focus on enjoying this person's company and at the same time protecting yourself from his or her frustrating qualities. Rather than spending family gatherings with your stomach knotted up, you *can* rise above the unpleasantness and hopefully enjoy some moments of closeness and warmth.

CHAPTER TWO

WHEN AND HOW TO CHANGE A FAMILY PATTERN YOU DON'T LIKE

Despite your best intentions, when interacting with difficult relatives there's always the chance of things turning ugly. It could be a family gathering where a certain cousin says something designed to rattle you. Or it might be an unpleasant phone conversation with a sibling that descends into harsh words or painful silences. Or it could be just the old familiar guilt dance or power struggle that you've done so many times before.

At those lovely moments, you may have wondered, "How did I let myself get drawn in again by this person? Am I a masochist or what?" Now ask yourself this: Wouldn't it be great to try something different instead—something that has a chance of changing a family pattern that has been causing you pain for too long?

In Chapter One, the focus was on using detachment and humor to break an old pattern and do some important inner work in response to a difficult family member. This chapter is about confronting the situation more directly. Here you'll learn when might be the right time to speak up or take action, what words and comeback lines can help and which ones tend to make things worse, and what kind of allies to enlist to improve your chances of being successful when you try to break old family patterns that you've disliked for many years.

AVOIDING THE MOST COMMON MISTAKES

Before figuring out what approach might work most effectively, it's important to identify what usually doesn't work. Specifically, there are three common responses to family tensions that frequently make things worse. See if you or someone in your family has made the mistake of trying one of the following.

The Tell-Them-Off Approach

In the late 1960s and early 1970s, it was fashionable for counselors to tell their clients to "release your anger," "let it all hang out," "tell them exactly how you feel," and "show them just how upset you are." If a counseling client came into a therapy session and said, "My manipulative sister-in-law hurt my feelings," the hip therapist with long, unkempt hair and extra-wide lapels would say, "You've got to tell her off. You've got to *express your feelings*."

Those were the days of pounding pillows, primal-scream

therapy, and hitting one another with rubber-coated bats called batacas. It was also a time when people wore paisley shirts, tie-dyed dresses, and roach clips as necklaces.

We've learned a lot since the days of the Mod Squad and Marcia Brady. Back then, advocates of "emotional catharsis" implied that you would feel less resentful, even blissful, after pouring out your anger. But scientific studies have taught us since that unloading on someone doesn't actually reduce the level of anger inside you but rather stirs up feelings of bitterness and revenge in both parties. Research suggests that in most cases, if you have a short fuse it's not likely to get any longer after you have verbally vomited on the other person.

To break out of the vicious cycle of attacking and counterattacking, watch closely the words you pick and the tone of voice you use. To avoid provoking your most difficult relative to become even more defensive or obnoxious, be sure to avoid sweeping accusations such as "You *always* do this" or "You *never* do that." As soon as you say the magic words "always" or "never," you can guarantee that your relative will stop listening and start defending himself.

Based on what I have observed in counseling hundreds of families, I would estimate that more than half of all fights happen because someone said the magic words "You *always*" or "You *never*." It's amazing how many conflicts can be avoided or improved just by eliminating those two words from your vocabulary.

The Constipated Approach

On the opposite extreme, there's a second mistake that many people make when dealing with their feelings. It happens when you try with all your might not to say or do anything in response to a crazy-making relative. Have you ever found yourself tightening your jaw and gritting your teeth while a pushy or obnoxious relative fills the room with his or her insensitivity? Have you felt your stomach twisting into knots or your chest tightening while a clique of domineering family members went on and on professing their version of reality? Have you felt helpless and frustrated that a family member was being rude, hurtful, or disrespectful?

I call this the constipated approach because that essentially describes what's taking place on a physiological level. This hold-it-all-in response is common among those who consider themselves good, nice, or decent. The difficult relative says or does unpleasant things and in response, the "nice" relative shuts down, holds his or her tongue, and feels all tensed up and blocked inside.

Quite often there are rationalizations that go along with the decision to clam up and do nothing. These rationalizations include the belief that if you keep silent you are taking the high road and acting more mature. Or maybe you have rationalized that if you placate or act compliantly toward the rude relative, he or she will eventually come to appreciate you more and treat you better. Fat chance.

If this sounds like you, please don't feel that you are the

only one who takes the constipated approach. We all have the tendency to rationalize from time to time. In fact, I remember in the 1983 film *The Big Chill*, when the journalist, played by Jeff Goldblum, asks his friends, "Which is more important—sex or rationalizations?" After a few seconds he answers, "When was the last time you went for a week without a rationalization?"

Most people who clam up when they are around a difficult relative also rationalize that they have nothing to lose by staying silent. But if you could take an MRI photograph of your jaw, your stomach, your intestines, your shoulders, and your heart and lungs at that moment you would see that you are causing quite a bit of internal upset with this constipated approach. Not only are you encouraging the difficult relative to treat you like a doormat, but you are also telling your vital organs, joints, and muscles that they are going to have to stay constricted with insufficient oxygen and sluggish bloodflow until some unspecified future time when hell freezes over and your relative miraculously starts to act differently. As they say in Brooklyn, don't be a putz.

The Passive-Aggressive Approach

Finally, there is a third response mode that most of us slip into every so often. Those inclined to use psychological jargon call it passive-aggressive behavior. In plain English, it's those times when we say to ourselves, "I won't say anything, I won't say anything, I won't say anything . . ." and then, on the fourth or fifth or tenth time that your difficult family member steps on your feelings, your anger squirts out in an unfortunate manner. The frustration you have been trying to keep locked inside might escape as sarcasm or as a vicious remark you later regret. Or you might start arguing forcefully in an attempt to convince this uncaring family member how wronged you feel, only to find that the relative is likely to respond in turn with defensiveness. You had tried so hard not to let your anger or hurt show and now you find yourself fully engaged after blurting out far more than you intended.

"They Kiss the Ground That He Walks On"

Carla's case is a good example of how hard it is to respond effectively to a difficult family member. As a sensitive and talented artist who pursues her art part-time while paying the bills by working as a production assistant in television, she admits she always felt a bit frustrated with her parents and three siblings, who have been trying to get Carla to stop being an artist and do something "realistic" like going to pharmacy school or business school. For years Carla simply tolerated her family get-togethers and tried to avoid the criticism of her family members. Carla said, "I love my family, even with all their conventional opinions and judgments. They're the only family I have, and we used to enjoy some wonderful moments in spite of our different lifestyles."

But eight years ago Carla's older sister Julie married a real estate broker named Kevin who takes great pleasure in poking fun at Carla and telling her how to fix her life. According to Carla, "There's something about Kevin's hostile jokes and invasive comments that cross the line for me. On several occasions Kevin has made fun of my looks, my boyfriends, my bank account, and my art to the extent that I had to walk out of a family gathering so as not to start crying in front of everyone. My family adores Kevin, probably because he makes mucho bucks, but also because he and my sister Julie are the first in the family to pop out the precious grandchildren my folks have wanted for a long time. So whenever I tell anyone in the family that Kevin is being hurtful or obnoxious, they look at me like I'm crazy. 'Who cares if he's a little intense sometimes?' they say. 'You're just being too sensitive.' It takes a lot to bring me to tears, but on several occasions Kevin has said things that really got me in a vulnerable place. I hate that he can do that to me."

Like many people who are forced into close contact with a painfully difficult relative every time they show up for a family event, Carla has attempted several things that haven't worked. She tried at first to tell Kevin off and found he got even more hurtful toward her in response. For a while she tried staying away from family gatherings, but she realized her absence was essentially a victory for Kevin. She then tried being polite and silent, hoping he might stop focusing on her. But this didn't work either, as Kevin made sure at every family event to find the right moment to say something that he knew would rattle Carla. Then Carla began to notice she had become passive-aggressive with him, trying hard to keep her frustration inside but instead stooping to his level every so often with sarcastic and vicious remarks that made each of her siblings turn to her and say, "Gosh, Carla, since when are you so edgy?"

When Carla first came in for counseling, she told me, "This can't go on. I don't want this creep to ruin every family event for me. But right now I dread seeing my family because I hate how they kiss the ground that he walks on. I feel like if it came down to a choice between siding with Kevin or siding with me, they'd definitely side with Kevin."

To help Carla change her approach to this painful situation, I started by focusing on Carla's own sense of self-worth. During our first few counseling sessions I worked with Carla to help her feel stronger about her gifts as an artist and her right to be different from the rest of her family. As Eleanor Roosevelt once said, "No one can make you feel inferior without your consent."

I had Carla make a list of all the people in her life who do appreciate her art, her humor, her kindness, her generosity, and her strength as a human being. As with many people who are outsiders in their families of origin, Carla soon understood, "I'm in trouble if I keep waiting for my family to tell me my artistic lifestyle has merit. I know they love me, even if they don't quite appreciate why I need to be different from them."

Over a period of weeks, and after joining a support

group of creative individuals, Carla came to realize that "I don't have to keep looking to my family for validation or approval of who I am. What I really want from our family get-togethers right now is to enjoy whatever moments of connection and warmth are possible while my parents are still alive. I've got to make sure Kevin's nonsense doesn't take that away from me."

MOVING FROM INTIMIDATION TO EMPATHY

Okay, so now that you know what *not* to do, what *can* you do to try to change a stressful pattern of interaction with a particular relative? The first and most powerful step is to change what you say to yourself about this person's obnoxiousness. For years Carla had viewed Kevin's criticisms and sarcastic remarks as being dangerous comments about her own inadequacies. To change this painful situation, I asked Carla to do some quick research. I urged her to find answers to a few important questions that you, too, should consider when dealing with your own difficult relatives.

What Could His Problem Be?

I suggested that Carla should ask around, "What happened in Kevin's early years that could have caused him to be so bitter and attacking?" When Carla talked to her sister Julie and one of Kevin's younger sisters about this, she learned some valuable information. When Kevin was very young he was considered unattractive and nerdy. In junior high and high school he was frequently rejected by the popular girls, and he got picked last in sports by the athletic team captains he had hoped to impress. Only in his thirties, when he began to make substantial money in real estate, did Kevin begin to blossom into someone who could find a date for Saturday night and have colleagues inviting him to play golf or tennis. Yet his insecurities and bitterness were probably still churning inside.

Does He or She Have a Nice Side?

What's your problem relative like when he or she's being nice? Granted, it may be tough to imagine him being fun, creative, affectionate, vulnerable, helpful, or kind when he picks on you all the time. Yet when Carla talked to her sister Julie and one of Kevin's old friends about this, she found out that Kevin did have a pleasant side to him. Julie told a story about when she was very ill, during the last four months of her difficult pregnancy with her second child. Kevin not only got up in the middle of the night and early in the morning to care for their older child, but he also brought flowers and prepared vitamin smoothies that he brought to Julie on a wooden "breakfast in bed" tray each morning. One of Kevin's longtime friends also mentioned that Kevin was often the only person to make a big deal out of various friends' birthdays. According to this friend, "We all know Kevin can be a complete jerk at times, but he's also loyal and dedicated to the people who are closest to him."

What about You Threatens This Individual?

This was the most helpful question Carla asked about Kevin. She had always thought of him as intimidating and threatening, so she couldn't imagine that he might in fact be threatened or intimidated by her. Then she had a heart-to-heart conversation one night on the phone with her sister Julie, during which Carla asked, "Is there something about me or the way I live my life that might be threatening to Kevin?"

Julie thought for a moment and responded, "That's an interesting question. I don't think I've ever told you that Kevin always wanted to be a musician. He worked real hard at it, and he played guitar in a cutting-edge band during high school and college. But they couldn't make much of a living from their music. So he stopped playing entirely. He hasn't picked up a guitar in over twelve years."

Carla thought she heard a touch of sadness in Julie's voice as Julie explained, "I guess Kevin feels uncomfortable and maybe even a little intimidated when he sees you sticking to your art. It probably makes him wonder if he gave up on his creative side too soon, or maybe he resents you for becoming what he couldn't become. Or maybe he thinks he's protecting you from the disappointment he suffered and that's why he's always trying to give you too much advice."

After finding out a little about Kevin, Carla felt the beginnings of a shift in the way she viewed him. As Carla told me in a counseling session, "I still don't like the guy, and I can't condone the way he talks to me. There ought to be a finishing school for adults where they teach basic human decency to guys like Kevin, who don't seem to understand the concept. But for the first time in many years I don't feel intimidated or as easily hurt by him anymore. I kinda feel sorry for him, and I'm glad he has a few friends and my sister Julie who understand his inner turmoil and his vulnerabilities."

The next week Carla saw Kevin at a family event, and she later told me how her perception has changed. "It feels different watching Kevin in action now after learning more about his past. There was a birthday dinner the other night for my mom and, as usual, Kevin made a stupid remark about what I was wearing. Yet it didn't have much of an impact on me this time. His immature comment was almost like static on the radio or someone expelling gas. Not pleasant, but not a very big deal. It felt like a breakthrough that I could watch him say something designed to upset me and I could remember that it was more about his insecurities than about mine."

As Carla and many of my counseling clients have discovered, even the most verbally abusive and intimidating person is usually mush inside. Like a cactus that has sharp needles on the outside to protect the soft, fragile inside, most of our difficult relatives have developed prickly layers and defensiveness to keep their inner psychological wounds a closely guarded secret.

I urge you to do some quick research and find out if the person who has caused you years of discomfort and pain is actually someone much more vulnerable than you've ever imagined. Instead of fearing this person or feeling inferior to him or her, it might be more appropriate to feel sadness or compassion.

FINDING THE RIGHT WORDS

Once Carla was no longer feeling intimidated by Kevin, I asked her if she would be willing to have a face-to-face conversation with him about improving their interactions. At first she was hesitant. She commented, "Why would I want to volunteer to spend an extra minute with this person when he's consistently so unpleasant?"

I explained to Carla that the goal of a face-to-face conversation is not to become roommates or best friends; nor is the goal to change this person's underlying personality or his way of being in the world. Rather, the goal is to see if there is a possibility for a small amount of improvement. In some family conflicts, the goal might be to make this person 10 percent less obnoxious, or to make it possible that a family get-together will be 20 percent more enjoyable. Even a small amount of progress will make your family holidays and gatherings that much less painful.

Carla was still hesitant. "I don't think there are any 'right words' to say to Kevin," she said. "He can turn whatever you say into another joke or another attack. He's impossible to talk with, and I don't relish the idea of putting myself out there for him to chop me up once again."

I offered Carla a choice, as I do with all my counseling clients who are unsure about whether to have a face-to-face conversation with an unpleasant family member. I told Carla, "If you decide not to talk to Kevin about how to improve things, I'll respect your decision. Taking good care of yourself by decreasing your contact with Kevin is a perfectly reasonable choice, especially if your intuition tells you there is no hope of any progress with him. On the other hand, I would love to explore what might be the right comeback lines for dealing with someone as verbally toxic as Kevin."

Carla thought for a few moments and said, finally, "I'm willing to give it a try." So we practiced a few comeback lines and nonthreatening phrases that might open Kevin up to making a slight improvement in the way he treats Carla at family events. Here are the words that have worked for many individuals. See if any of these feel right to you for your particular situation.

Asking for Help

If you want to soften someone's calloused heart and build better rapport with a relative who has been very harsh or difficult in the past, one of the gentlest and most effective phrases is to say, "You and I both want our family gatherings to be more enjoyable and less stressful. I need your help and your advice. Tell me what you think will make things a little better the next time we get together for a family event."

You will notice that these disarming, nonthreatening

words put aside the past. They bypass the personality clashes. They avoid troublesome words like "always" and "never." They are a direct invitation for the other person to start thinking positively and constructively about how to improve things.

This technique was developed many years ago by experts and consultants who advise companies on how to deal with irate customers. Instead of arguing with an angry customer or telling him to "Lower your voice" or "Don't be so angry"—two phrases that often cause the angry person to start shouting even louder—the most effective response is to calmly ask the upset individual to explain slowly and carefully what advice he or she would give you to improve the situation. By letting the other person speak first, and by listening to each idea or suggestion with seriousness and respect, you will turn an angry adversary into a more relaxed and cooperative individual. The best customer service representatives and customer relations professionals are the ones who can listen so caringly and attentively that the irate customer instinctively knows it's time to calm down.

This same technique works extremely well with angry, stubborn, or obnoxious family members. If you make the mistake of saying "Lower your voice" or "Calm down," your relative will probably shout even louder. On the other hand, if you imagine yourself to be a powerful and well-trained customer relations specialist who knows how to defuse and calm an irate and verbally provocative customer, you can see yourself not as a helpless victim but rather as a competent and caring professional. With the calmest and most respectful voice you can muster, you might then say, "You and I both want our family gatherings to be more enjoyable and less stressful. I need your help and your advice. Tell me what you think will make things a little better the next time we get together for a family event."

If the difficult family member doesn't immediately come around, just keep imagining yourself to be a powerful and well-trained customer relations expert. Calmly and warmly remind the other person, "I'm listening. I do want to understand what you're telling me. What do you think will make things better?" By managing and directing the conversation in this way, you keep it positive and goal-oriented. It might look like you are being soft or compliant, but in fact you are taking charge. Sooner or later, even the most difficult family member is likely to offer some ideas on how to make the next family event less stressful.

Here's what happened when Carla tried out this first phrase with Kevin. Carla called him on the phone one evening and asked if he had a minute to offer her some advice. Kevin jumped at the chance. Then she repeated the phrase we had practiced: "You and I both want our family gatherings to be more enjoyable and less stressful. I need your help and your advice. Tell me what you think will make things a little better the next time we get together for a family event."

At that point, Kevin made an obnoxious and sarcastic remark, telling Carla, "It'll be a lot better if you lose ten pounds and you wear a dark thong under a see-through dress."

But Carla didn't take the bait. Staying calm and strong, she said simply, "Well, that's one idea to consider. And I know we both want things to improve at our family events. I do need your help and your advice. What do you think might improve things?"

Kevin was quiet for a moment. Then he listed six different things that he thought would make the next family event less stressful for everyone. As Carla told me a few days later, "Some of Kevin's ideas were ridiculous, but I just listened respectfully and let him know I was taking him seriously. Surprisingly, a few of his ideas were pretty good. I told him I liked one of his ideas a lot. That seemed to soften him a bit. I never realized it before, but it's quite possible that Kevin desperately wants me to like him and approve of him. But he's got an awfully bizarre way of trying to win me over. He's like one of those nine-year-old boys who punches his friend in the arm or the stomach as a way of bonding or getting closer. As Kevin and I talked for several minutes about his ideas and my ideas on how to improve things in our family, I got the sense that he had wanted this kind of closeness for many years but he'd done all the wrong things to try to get me to like him. What a sad situation that people in our families want to connect but they do the very things that will make connection impossible."

A few weeks later there was another family event, and Carla said she was anxious to see if there would be any improvement as a result of her phone conversation with Kevin. "For the first few hours everything went fine. Kevin was more civil and less obnoxious than I've ever seen him. But true to form, he did make a couple of hurtful comments near the end of the evening. I'd say overall it was a 50 percent improvement."

As Carla's story illustrates, the goal is not to change your relative completely or to expect a 100 percent improvement. But if you initiate a conversation where both you and the other person can brainstorm on how to make things better at your family events, you will probably see at least a little benefit.

The Caring Sandwich

Ideally you will never have to ask for anything from your most difficult family member. But sometimes you do need this person to help you out and there's no getting around it.

For example, one afternoon Carla came into my office and told me she unfortunately needed something very important from Kevin and she was unsure of how to talk to him about it. She was planning to bring her new boyfriend, Roger, to an upcoming holiday dinner that she was hoping would be a positive first meeting for Roger and her family. She had warned Roger about Kevin, but still she was worried that Kevin might somehow go out of his way to ruin this important holiday gathering.

As Carla described it, "I've begun to have anxious thoughts in the middle of the night about bringing Roger to meet my crazy family for the first time. It's risky because I think Roger might be more than just another boyfriend. It feels like he might be my future husband, unless my family or something else starts to drive us apart. So I don't want Kevin saying things about me to Roger that will humiliate me. And I would prefer if Roger got to meet my entire family at an event that goes well, instead of the usual fiasco where ugly scenes and hurtful words leave everyone feeling badly."

While I reminded Carla that there is no guarantee of being able to change or control a difficult relative, especially someone as habitually rude and insensitive as Kevin, we did explore a second way of approaching Kevin that has been effective for many of my counseling clients. Though it doesn't always succeed, it can help get your needs considered more seriously and may encourage your difficult relative to be at his or her best behavior at least for a short time after your talk.

I call this powerful but nonthreatening communication technique the Caring Sandwich because it consists of two caring comments surrounding and buffering an assertive statement or request in the middle. Once you understand the concept, you can utilize this approach whenever you're being assertive and asking for something specific from a difficult relative.

The Caring Sandwich that Carla and I developed for getting Kevin to control himself and be less obnoxious at the upcoming holiday gathering had three parts:

"I Respect You"

As the name suggests, the Caring Sandwich has a bottom, a middle, and a final component to top it all off. The bottom, or foundation, of the Caring Sandwich is the positive statement you make in order to soften the calloused heart of this difficult relative. Start out by mentioning some aspect of this person's life that you admire or enjoy. Even if you don't like most of what you know about this troubled individual, it's crucial that you find something positive and true to say as the first part of your request.

In Carla's case, the Caring Sandwich began with her calling up Kevin a few hours before the family event to which she would be bringing Roger. After asking Kevin how his family was doing, Carla said, "Kevin, I respect you for being a great husband to my sister and an amazing dad with your two kids. I know you've got a good heart."

Note that Carla said these words with sincerity and genuineness. It's very important that the foundation of your Caring Sandwich be made with positive statements that you feel are true, or else you will sound insincere and manipulative. If you have trouble coming up with anything positive or caring about your difficult relative, you may need to ask others to help you find the spark of goodness and decency that exists deep inside even the most unpleasant human beings but may get thoroughly covered over by layers and layers of difficult traits and habits.

"I Really Hope You'll Say Only Positive Things about Me"
The next words out of your mouth must be a gentle and clear request explaining what you need this person to do. Without accusing, attacking, blaming, or lecturing, you simply need to find a few brief words that describe exactly what you hope he or she will do this time to prevent a painful incident. In Carla's case, the middle portion of her Caring Sandwich was the direct but tactful request, "I need your help on something very important. I'm bringing a new person to the holiday dinner and I really hope you'll say only positive things about me and the family so that my friend Roger will have a good impression of all of us."

"I Know You Can Do This"
The final words out of your mouth should be a positive, supportive comment that you are confident this person can and will come through today. It's like a pep talk from an encouraging coach. In Carla's phone conversation with Kevin, she said, "I know you can do this. I've seen your caring and your compassion. I hope you can help me out and make today a good event without any friction."

By carefully constructing your Caring Sandwich, what you say can focus your family member on doing the right thing at a family event.

Here's what happened at Carla's holiday gathering. While driving with Roger to the event, she explained in greater detail some of the past difficulties she'd had with Kevin and what her quick research had taught her about some of the sources of Kevin's insecurities and hostile comments. Roger listened carefully and then replied, "Don't worry. I'm not going to freak because you've got some difficult people in your family. I've got some real characters in my family, too. I promise not to hold you responsible for any disasters that happen at a family event. That's what families are all about. And as for Kevin, if he says anything obnoxious about you, I'll just have one of my cousins arrange a hit on him." When Carla looked at him after that comment, Roger smiled and said, "Just kidding."

At the event, Kevin was more cautious and restrained than usual. Carla told me later that Kevin almost seemed to be trying to win her approval. "He did make a few obnoxious jokes about political figures and the private lives of motion picture stars, but for the first time in years he avoided saying anything hostile toward me."

Every situation and every family is slightly different. You may find when using the Caring Sandwich that it works beautifully some of the time to help a difficult family member take your needs more seriously. But at other times your relative's troubled personality or self-centeredness might reveal itself once again no matter what you do or say. What's most important about the Caring Sandwich, however, is that it doesn't make things worse. It's a nonthreatening way to be assertive without provoking a new round of attacks and counterattacks. It gets the other person's attention and invites him or her to be a cooperative ally, at least for a short amount of time. If you practice using it, you will find it is one of the most effective ways of bringing out the best in people who otherwise seem intent on showing off their most awful traits.

RESPONDING TO WORST-CASE SCENARIOS

In some cases there is nothing you can say to sway certain family members. It might be a moody teenager who stubbornly refuses to listen to anything you say, or a self-absorbed parent or in-law who chronically lacks the ability to take your needs seriously or empathize with your point of view. Or it might be a dogmatic or self-righteous relative who habitually refuses to see that there are two sides to every family conflict, or a psychologically wounded member of your family who often cannot hear even your gentlest comments without feeling highly insulted or becoming instantly defensive.

What can you do when this difficult relative has closed you out and yet you need some amount of cooperation from him or her? What might resolve this impasse without making matters worse? Here are two options to consider when things get especially nasty.

Let Go

What if you were to give up all expectations that this person might be different? What if you were to let go of the idea that he or she can be changed or improved?

This may sound pessimistic, but oftentimes if you completely stop trying to change, outsmart, or manipulate your difficult family member, some interesting things happen. You free yourself from having to be this person's judge, jailer, or rehabilitation coach. You also will feel relief at not having to work so hard to get along with this person. Your brain can stop trying so desperately to "figure it out" if you sincerely let go of all efforts to change this individual.

What does it mean to let go? If you are a spiritual or religious person, you may find that a renewed sense of clarity and strength emerges if you stop strategizing for a while and instead pray, meditate, or visualize in silence. Extensive research over the past twenty years has demonstrated that if you let yourself breathe gently in silence to attain a peaceful acceptance of a painful situation that is beyond your control, you sometimes can reach a higher awareness about what's really going on. A sense of divine healing energy or deep intuitive clarity may allow you to break out of your agitation and help you attain some new insights about the situation in your family. I have found repeatedly in my own life and with many of my counseling clients that sitting in silence and focusing on the breath, or on a vision of warm healing light from a higher source, can bring new creativity to the problem of dealing with life's toughest challenges.

Yet if you are not comfortable with terms like divine healing energy, higher source, or peaceful acceptance, there is also a scientific/psychological explanation for this same phenomenon of letting go in order to see things more clearly. Twenty-five years ago, a brilliant Gestalt psychologist and prominent researcher from UCLA named Arnold Beisser developed and studied the effectiveness of something he called *the paradoxical theory of change*.

Beisser asked a number of men and women who were dealing with a difficult challenge to imagine themselves relaxed, calm, and centered while *not* trying to change the problem whatsoever. These individuals practiced the art of letting go, fully accepting that they were in the middle of a painful and upsetting situation that they couldn't control. Based on his research, Beisser concluded that the best way to change a painful situation is first to become centered, calm, and unhurried about where you are, at least for a few moments. Giving your mind and body a brief sabbatical will open up new avenues of insight and creative perspective. Beisser's theory has been used successfully by hundreds of therapists and thousands of counseling clients over the years.

Since I am originally from snowy Michigan and also lived in the northeastern United States for a number of years, I think of Beisser's theory in terms of how to get your car out of a one- or two-foot pile of snow. Experienced northerners can tell you that if you aggressively put your car in drive, press your foot hard on the accelerator pedal, and "go for it," you only get deeper into a snowy rut. Your wheels spin and you go nowhere. But if you calmly accept that you are in a rut and you gently rock your car back and forth, back and forth, between reverse and forward, your vehicle usually finds enough traction to move out of the snowy trap. It's not about racing forward, but rather about calmly assessing the spot you are in. In a similar way, using prayer, meditation, guided visualization, or Beisser's paradoxical theory of change during a painful family conflict can provide you with the necessary traction, patience, and gentleness for transforming a situation where forceful action often makes things worse.

So whether you think of letting go as a spiritual practice or a psychological/scientific technique, it can be highly effective in helping us break out of old ruts to see things from a new and more innovative perspective.

"The More We Tried, the Bigger the Wall He Put Up to Shut Us Out"

What if you had a troubled relative who consistently lied to you, ignored your good advice, and tried to manipulate you? What if you had been trying for years to make an impact on this person and each time you felt completely thwarted?

I once suggested the let-go approach to a counseling client of mine named Corey, a twenty-nine-year-old licensed social worker who had spent many years feeling frustrated from trying to "fix" his troubled younger brother, Philip, twenty-seven, an extremely charismatic but highly elusive and manipulative individual who had been in and out of jail several times for using and selling drugs. Corey and his parents had tried nearly everything to help Philip: tough love, expensive treatment centers, various pharmacological remedies, daily phone calls, and prominent drug counseling experts. Corey told me that nearly every day he felt upset and burdened by the mess Philip had made of his life. But, Corey said, "The more we tried, the bigger the wall he put up to shut us out."

Corey was surprised when I asked him, "What would happen if you stopped for a few days or a few weeks and simply let go of the need to change your brother? What if you *had* to accept him exactly as he is? I realize letting go is not an easy thing to do, but if you were to use prayer, meditation, or guided visualization, you might be able to see your brother not as a stubborn problem to be fixed, but somehow in a new and different light."

"Are you saying I should become passive and just let my brother's situation worsen?"

"No," I said, "I'm not saying to be passive or to abandon your brother. If you learn to let go, something happens inside the mind when we stop trying to figure things out and we just breathe in and out calmly while accepting things exactly how they are with no agitation or impatience. If you are willing to practice using prayer, meditation, or visualization to get beyond your frustration and irritation, you might open yourself up to new and highly effective ways of seeing the issue with your brother."

Although he was a bit skeptical, Corey said he was willing to try this approach. Over a period of several weeks he began sitting in silence for ten minutes each day with the intention of opening up his heart and his mind to a different way of looking at the situation with his younger brother. Corey admitted this wasn't easy. "Most of the time when I sit in silence, my brain starts racing with thoughts and angry feelings about my brother and how much I want to tell him what to do."

I assured Corey that this "brain noise" is a normal response and that everyone who prays, meditates, or uses guided visualization finds his or her mind drifting, especially in the early stages of learning how to let go. When you notice your mind racing, it doesn't mean you're doing anything wrong. It just means you should go back to noticing your breath moving softly in and out of your body as you go deeper into silence.

Corey decided to stick with the ten-minutes-a-day routine, and after a few weeks he did experience a higher percentage of peaceful moments. Then, during one of these silent sessions, something unusual happened.

Corey told me during his next counseling appointment, "I was sitting in my room, meditating with less brain noise than usual, and I started to envision a memory of a warm sunny day where my brother Philip and I were just relaxing at the beach. At that moment, I sensed a deep connection with Philip and I noticed a few tears in my eyes."

Corey continued, "It sounds strange, but the feeling I had was that on some level Philip and I aren't really separate

beings who are at odds with each other. I don't know exactly
how to say this, but it was as though Philip and I share a deep
soul connection, almost like we're part of the same whole. It's
hard to explain, but for an instant I felt completely at peace
with who he is, and I had this thought that Philip's path in life
and my path in life are somehow meant to be. I began to feel
so much less judgmental of him and all he's been going
through. After years of wanting to grab him and shake him, I
had a moment of feeling a lot of love and acceptance for my
kid brother. It was the first time I saw him as a pure soul
who's trapped inside a very addicted body. And then I imagined Philip looking me in the eye and saying, 'Don't judge
me, Corey. In this lifetime I acquired the messed-up biochemistry. In the next lifetime, it could be you with the addictive urges, and in that lifetime you might need my support
and patience.'"

That meditation experience was the beginning of a
breakthrough in Corey's relationship with Philip. As Corey
describes it, "There are still challenging moments, but something changed in the way I've talked to him ever since that
silent meditation when I felt our connection in a new way.
Philip tells me I no longer sound as impatient, judgmental, or
self-righteous as I apparently had become toward him for
many years. Now when we talk on the phone or see each
other in person, he says he feels like I'm an ally instead of a
'patronizing asshole.' So he's begun to let down the wall that
he'd put up for a long time. That's not to say things are per-

fect with Philip. I still wouldn't feel safe lending him money or letting him babysit my infant daughter. Philip's still battling his inner turmoil, his drug cravings, and I can sense at times he's still tempted to go back to his lifelong habit of manipulating people."

A few weeks later, Corey told me during his final office visit, "The good news is that Philip's been drug free for twenty-six days so far, but I don't know what will happen. Whether he stays clean or not is beyond my control. Yet lately he's been real honest with me and we've gotten very close, like brothers again. The shift in the way I see him has helped us stop getting on each other's nerves so much."

Can letting go through a technique such as prayer, meditation, or guided visualization cause a breakthrough in your relationship with an extremely difficult relative? I have seen that for some counseling clients it has made a huge difference, while for others nothing much seems to happen.

In Corey's case, learning to let go not only helped him become less judgmental and more successful with his brother, but it also helped Corey become a less rigid and more effective social worker. As Corey told me in a phone call a year after he completed his counseling sessions, "I realize now that I used to be a bit too self-righteous and impatient with my social work families. Just like I was somewhat patronizing and judgmental with Philip, I was that way in my professional life as well. Letting go with Philip taught me how to connect on a more profound level with the families I'm trying to help in my work."

I have found that quite often the hard-earned lessons we gain from fully accepting our difficult family members help us in other areas of our lives as well. The struggle to overcome our own impatience and rigidity in our family interactions often leads to less impatience and rigidity in our work and even our romantic relationships. You might want to think of your frustrations with your relatives as being like the abrasive sand in an oyster's shell that helps create a valuable and stunning pearl. We don't know ahead of time what kind of growth or pearl will emerge from these encounters, but in hindsight, they often are important breakthroughs.

Each person reading this book has to decide for herself whether she really wants to try to fully accept her family members as vulnerable human beings. Each reader has to look inside and make his own assessment of whether he wants to explore spiritual, religious, or unconventional techniques as a possible option when things get nasty with a relative. I can't tell you what to do, but I hope you will check in with your own spiritual, religious, or psychological advisors, along with books, teachers, and your own inner feelings, to find out what might work for you in dealing with difficult family members.

Call for Back-Up

Besides letting go, another option that can help break an impasse with an especially stubborn relative is what I refer to as calling for back-up. In many family conflicts, a relative may not listen to you but he or she will listen to someone who has a certain power or authority.

It could be a minister, priest, or rabbi who can call, write, or talk in person to your difficult relative and say, "I'm concerned about your family and I need you to do the right thing and be a good person here." Or it could be the best friend of your problem relative, who can look him or her in the eye and say, "Cut the crap." It might be an elder in the family who has enough status and influence to be able to say, "Stop it right now." Or it might be a counselor, lawyer, accountant, advisor, physician, social worker, or other professional person who has enough of a track record and enough clout with your difficult relative to be able to say, "Listen to me. This is what you need to do."

In the field of family therapy, this calling for assistance is considered a controversial approach. Throughout the past three decades, there has been a trend in the profession against what is called *triangulation*, psych jargon that means if you are Person A and you have a conflict with Family Member B, you mustn't expect Person C to speak up on your behalf or solve the problem with Family Member B for you. Some family therapists think that talking to Person C when you have a problem with Family Member B is weak or manipulative. A few family therapists absolutely forbid their counseling clients to ask an outsider for assistance. These therapists believe we must fight our own battles and confront face-to-face the people in our family who have wronged us. They insist that unless you talk to Family Member B directly and resolve the problem on your own, you will not be fully healed or empowered.

While I agree that as a general rule it's preferable to deal with people directly and not to go behind their backs, there are certain family conflicts and crises that require a different approach. For example, Rita's case is a clear illustration of when it's appropriate and extremely effective to call for backup. If you have a relative as difficult as Rita's mom, you might want to consider using a similar approach.

"She's a Real Piece of Work"

Barbara is Rita's mom. A very attractive, stylish, and intelligent sixty-two-year-old woman with a fiery temper, Barbara has been divorced three times. When you first meet her, you notice how cultured and charming she can be. Barbara has two living children, Rita, thirty-three, and a younger son, Bruce, thirty-one, who moved several years ago to New Zealand. Barbara's first child, Gayle, died in a car accident almost twenty years ago, an event that still weighs heavily on the family.

My counseling client Rita is the program director at a nonprofit agency that helps homeless and battered women find shelter, clothes, job training, better incomes, and increased self-worth. Rita and her fiancé, Eric, have been together for three years, and they decided seven months ago to get married.

According to Rita, "Eric and I knew when we started to plan our wedding that my mom was going to be difficult. But we had no idea it would get this hairy. My mother says to her friends that she's proud of my work with homeless and battered women, and yet she gets extremely upset and vindictive every time she calls my cell phone and doesn't get an immediate answer. She'll either stop talking to me for a week or she'll call a couple hours later and say, 'You are the most uncaring daughter. I called you at four o'clock and you didn't even pick up the phone. Where were you?'"

Whenever her mother chews her out for not picking up the phone, Rita feels caught in a no-win situation. She explains, "If I tell my mom I was in a meeting, my mother will either slam the phone down or else stay on the line and say tearfully, 'I thought you were dead.'" Rita admits, "When she does that, I'm never sure if my mom is truly feeling the pain from when my sister Gayle died in a car accident or whether my mom is just being dramatic and controlling. It's very hard to know with my mother whether you should feel compassion for her pain or whether you should be protecting yourself against her manipulations."

A few weeks before Rita's wedding, an incident occurred that brought Rita into counseling. Rita and Eric had decided that they wanted to invite Rita's father (Barbara's first husband) to be a part of the wedding. Rita told me, "He is my father and I do love him a lot. Even though he and my mom have hated each other for years, I felt I wanted him to be included at this important gathering. But I also knew this might send my mom into a tailspin, so Eric and I took my mother out to a nice restaurant and explained to her very respectfully how we want this to be a good event for her, too. And we asked her in the nicest way if there was any possibility she could be okay with my father being at the wedding at a separate table and having a lesser role in the ceremony."

According to Rita, "I never saw my mother get so hurt and upset as she was right then. She stormed out of the restaurant and has refused to talk to me ever since, except to leave a message on my voice mail to say she will not be attending my wedding. I don't know what to do. Part of me says to just let my mom make her own choices and hope that the wedding will be fine without her. Part of me says I need to apologize or suck up for a while because it will feel strange to have a huge family gathering, with my relatives flying in from all over, and my mom not there. If I think about what I really want in the big picture, it's very clear to me—I want to find a way to get my mother to show up and behave herself at my wedding. But whenever I try to call my mom to talk about this, she hangs up on me. How do I break through her wall?"

When I explored with Rita if there was anything she could do or say differently to help her mother show up at the wedding, Rita explained to me that "my mom is very prideful. If she says she's not coming to the wedding, there's nothing I can do to change her mind. Besides, she won't talk to me on the phone and she sent back the loving card I sent her last week. She's a real piece of work, my mom."

I then asked Rita, "Is there anyone in your mom's inner circle that might be able to talk to her and help her calm down between now and the wedding?" Rita thought for a moment and came up blank.

So I suggested, "Is there a member of the clergy who has some influence with your mom?" Rita laughed and said, "My mother gives some money to one particular guy who I don't think is likely to stand up to her or take my side. I wish he was the kind of inspiring leader who could help my mom live up to the high-integrity principles he talks about in his sermons, but right now the congregation is totally focused on raising money to build a new facility and I can't imagine this particular guy is gonna risk alienating someone like my mom by confronting her."

I then asked, "Are there any relatives who, because of age or family tradition, have some clout with your mom?" Rita smiled and said, "There's no one in the family who hasn't had a falling out with her. Believe me, if there were someone my mother would listen to, I'd gladly ask them to help out."

So I inquired, "Does your mom have a friend with whom she discusses things and who might be helpful?" Rita replied, "My mother has several women she goes with to museums or movies or concerts. But I know for a fact they don't give her advice. In fact, one of her friends told me recently, 'Your mom is a very smart woman when it comes to fashion and culture. But I never make the mistake of talking about personal relationships or family issues with her. She invariably gets upset and that can ruin things for the rest of the time we're together.'"

I was almost ready to give up, but then I said, "Can you think of anyone at all who isn't afraid of your mom?" Rita's face lit up a bit and she told me, "There is one person who has always been able to talk back to my mom and get away with it. My mom has had the same cleaning woman for almost twenty years. But she's a lot more than a cleaner. Maria's like a surrogate mother for my mom, and she's been a consistent source of stability in my mother's life. Maria's tough and I know she survived a horrible dictatorship in Central America. So she doesn't back down when my mom pisses her off. I've seen Maria tell my mom to chill out. I've seen her tease my mom about eating too many carbohydrates, and one time she even stood up to my mom and told her she was being 'a bitch on four wheels.' Maria can say things to my mother that I could never say or get away with."

So Rita arranged a private meeting with Maria and asked her, "Would you be willing to talk to my mother and help her be decent at my wedding, even if her ex-husband is in the room?" Maria smiled and said, "Damn right I'll do it. I think it's disgraceful that Barbara has been acting like this. Of course I'll be happy to talk to her. I'm even going to bring my wedding photo album from home and my daughter's wedding photo album. I'm gonna show your mother how important these family photos are and let her know how often my grandchildren look at them. Believe me, I don't think Barbara is going to want to be left out of the pictures. This is about much more than just an ex-husband, and Barbara needs to wake up and realize what she's gonna miss."

In every family situation there is almost always someone who has the clout to stand up and be effective with even the most intimidating or stubborn relative. If you can't think of who this might be regarding your difficult family member, ask around: "Who might be the one person that has some influence or sway with _____?"

Several weeks later, Rita and Eric got married. The photographer took mostly candid shots of the dancing, the celebration, the rituals, and the joy. But there were also several posed shots of the important members of Rita's immediate and extended family, and Barbara was right there in the middle of those photos, looking great after spending substantial time and money getting her hair, her nails, her skin, her dress, and her jewelry just right.

As Rita said afterward, "It was a fantastic wedding, and my mom knew she needed to behave herself. Very few people at the event had any idea how much drama had taken place leading up to that memorable day. I love my mom and I hate my mom. But I'm glad she was there at my wedding."

CHAPTER THREE

FIVE WAYS TO IMPROVE FAMILY GET-TOGETHERS AND HOLIDAY VISITS

Each year brings family holidays, religious holidays, secular holidays, and other special occasions for relatives to gather. At these events, will your family get along or get on each other's nerves? Will you come away with great memories or frustration headaches?

If the only thing you knew about family gatherings was what you saw depicted in magazine ads and television specials, you might imagine that all across America, men and women are sitting down to lovely, stress-free meals with well-behaved relatives. You might have the impression that family celebrations are satisfying and a joy for all those in attendance.

But if you were to tell the truth about what really happens when *your* extended family gets together for birthdays, coming-of-age ceremonies, weddings, and the like, you might recall that there are moments when certain relatives get on your nerves. If you think back to your last few family gatherings for Thanksgiving, Hanukah, Christmas, Kwanzaa, Easter,

Passover, Mother's Day, Father's Day, or other traditional holidays, is there some aspect that has needed fixing for many years? Is there some part of a family get-together that leaves you with a bad feeling each time, and yet it keeps getting repeated over and over again?

This chapter will focus on how to change the specific elements that need improvement at your family gatherings, and what can be done to make these important events far more enjoyable and less stressful. Based on the ideas I've acquired from listening to the collective wisdom of thousands of families who have come into my office or attended one of my seminars, I would like to offer a few practical tips for you to consider.

But first, have you ever heard the story about the extra-tender pot roast? Whether you are a vegetarian or a meat lover, this story is about more than just food.

A young woman named Gina, who was going to be hosting a large family gathering, wanted to learn how to make a tender pot roast (because her relatives expect pot roast at big family events and Gina's only previous attempt had turned out dry and tough). So she asked her mother for advice on how to make the perfect pot roast, and her mother said, "You have to cut off the tip—exactly like my own mother always did—and make sure the roast isn't too large. That's the secret for keeping in the juices and making it tender." Then Gina's mom pulled out a gourmet chef's knife and showed Gina precisely how to cut off the tip of the roast before putting it in a special pan and cooking it.

Gina did exactly what her mother suggested, but her pot roast came out dry and tough again. So Gina decided to ask her grandmother, who said, "You just need to cut a little more off the tip. That's what your great-grandmother always did and her roasts were so moist and tender."

This time Gina carefully did just what her grandmother told her to do, but once again the pot roast came out somewhat tough and dry. So she decided to spend some time with her beloved great-grandmother. Gina said to her, "I want to make an extra tender pot roast—do I need to cut off more of the tip?"

Her great-grandmother laughed and remarked, "You think that would help?"

Gina replied, "Well, Mom and Grandma both said that's how you always did it, and your roasts were amazingly tender."

The great-grandmother laughed again. "Gina, honey, do you know why I cut off the tip? I had a very small roaster pan . . . no other reason. If you want a tender pot roast, cook it slowly at 275 degrees for six hours and it'll be plenty tender."

As in this pot roast story, quite often our families don't remember exactly why an "essential" family holiday routine or habit first got started. Like the mother and grandmother in the story, we keep doing the barely understood routine and we assume it's the only way to do things. It takes someone like Gina to go and find out precisely why her family has been cutting off the tip of the meat for more than sixty years.

This chapter will seek to uncover if you and your family

have been following a similarly misguided notion of what your relatives think will make things tender at family events. Rather than continuing to rely on some outdated habit or family myth that hasn't worked effectively for years, there will be five specific alternatives offered for making sure you come away from family gatherings far more satisfied and far less frustrated.

WAY #1: SHORTEN THE LENGTH OF GET-TOGETHERS

Quite often after hearing from friends, colleagues, and counseling clients that they had a disappointing time at a family event or vacation visit with their relatives, I ask two questions: "How long were things relatively peaceful before they began to turn sour?" and "What is your family tradition for the length of a 'proper' stay?"

If you take a moment to think of the answers that apply to your own family gatherings, you might be surprised to find you've hit upon one of the most prevalent causes of family conflicts: Your family visits might be lasting longer than you and your relatives can handle.

I learned about this phenomenon firsthand several years ago when I was supervising my son's play dates with his friends. As many parents discover from experience, if you schedule a preschooler's play date for an hour or two, the kids get along well enough. But if you schedule the get-together for too much longer—say, three or four hours for kids that young—then fights, crankiness, and stubbornness are bound to occur.

It's the same way for families. During a summer vacation or winter break visit, you and your relatives might tend to get along pretty well for the first three or four days. But if your family has a rock-solid tradition of spending ten days or two weeks together and it usually ends up in fights, well then, let's face facts: The play date is too long. Or if experience tells you that a three-hour holiday gathering or festive meal goes somewhat smoother than a seven-hour marathon with four hours of pre-meal cocktails and appetizer small talk, you don't need an advanced degree in psychology to figure out that maybe the three-hour gathering might be the better idea.

Lobbying for Change

Here's the catch: It may be easier to pass an amendment to the Constitution than to change one of these "we've always done it this way" family routines. If you were to call your parents, your in-laws, or your other relatives and say, "Hey, I read this pop psych book by some bald-headed therapist who said that maybe we'd be better off having a peaceful three-hour Thanksgiving [or Hanukah or Christmas dinner] rather than sticking with our seven-hour version, where people drink far too much and become difficult"—in most families that would land you in deep trouble very quickly. How dare you change the way it's been done as far back as anyone can remember? How dare you question the family tradition?

Clearly, these kinds of earth-shattering changes do not usually get accomplished with just one phone call. You may need to lobby for months with several of your family members to build a consensus that maybe it's time to focus on what works and stop repeating what doesn't. In the families that have successfully changed family gatherings from "way too long" to "just right," it usually took the following specific steps.

1. After a family holiday event or visit that got ugly because it went on too long, be sure to call up the sanest members of the family and ask them if they also thought the event was a bit lengthy. Did they notice the three relatives who in the fourth hour got so drunk or overstuffed that their personalities changed or they fell asleep? Did they find that certain testy relatives were able to stay civil for a limited amount of time, but because the event was so long the civility began to melt away until the nasty arguments and power struggles began to reemerge? Did anyone observe how the young children in the family did pretty well the first portion of the gathering but were unable to keep it together past a certain point? Did anyone else think that if the event had ended after X number of hours it would have inspired good memories instead of the painful ones that everyone had? Helping your relatives begin to consider the time element is a crucial first step.

2. Next, you may want to brainstorm with your sanest relatives to decide which of you will be the key spokespeople advocating a change for next time. Which of you has the guts

or willingness to speak up? Which of you has the respect and influence in your extended family to get the elders and most powerful family members to see your point of view? How many of your sanest relatives are willing to volunteer to talk gently and lovingly to the one member of the family whom you can anticipate ahead of time will act "crushed" and "devastated" by even the possibility of changing the family routine?

3. Finally, when you pitch this new idea to the one or two family members who might feel threatened by the notion of changing anything, be sure to tell them that this is not necessarily a permanent change but rather an experiment. Explain it this way: "We'll see how it goes. If it doesn't improve anything, we can go back to the longer version. If it does improve things, we can discuss whether to run the experiment a second time or just go back to the traditional version." This promise of a one-time experiment must be sincere, though. If, after giving it a chance, your reluctant relative doesn't think there's been enough improvement, then you may have to compromise and let the old ways prevail.

"Way Too Many Drinks and Appetizers"

I once counseled a woman named Evelyn who told me, "In my family it's traditional for every Thanksgiving, Christmas, and Easter to be a seven-hour event. The cousins, aunts, uncles, grandparents, in-laws, and other relatives show up at my mother-in-law's house around two P.M. and we spend the next four hours having way too many drinks and appetizers, until by the time dinner is served around six P.M., the scene has gotten very unmanageable. The kids are out of control, the grown-ups are exhausted, and the three problem drinkers in the family are getting long-winded or quick-tempered."

Evelyn described how "for years we begged my mother-in-law to make it shorter or serve the meal earlier. But each time she would start crying and say, 'This is how it was in my family when I was a little girl. We came at two o'clock and we ate at six o'clock. How can you ask me to give up one of my favorite memories from my childhood?'"

Evelyn told me she was very frustrated at her mother-in-law's repeated inflexibility. She also said, "My mother-in-law is totally rewriting history. We all know there was serious alcoholism and even some abuse in her family. But my mother-in-law can sit there and say with a completely straight face, 'Don't make me change how wonderful it was when I was a little girl.'"

In many families, there is a myth about how the holidays were perfect long ago. That need not be your concern. Many of our relatives live in that heavily populated fifty-first state, the state of denial, and you can't force them to give up their rewritten memories. Our difficult and troubled relatives are going to remember the past in whatever ways suit them, truthful or not.

But what helped Evelyn's mother-in-law to loosen up a bit was for Evelyn, Evelyn's husband, his sister, and one other sibling to offer a one-time experiment. In a calm and nonthreatening tone of voice at a family dinner two months before the holidays, Evelyn and these other members of her husband's family suggested to Evelyn's mother-in-law, "We're not asking for a permanent change in the holiday tradition. Let's just try an experiment this one time. Let's have a meal where we all pitch in and help you out. People can come at four P.M. and we'll serve dinner by five-thirty. Then we'll have a look to see if the children, the feuders, the problem drinkers, and the others do better this time. If it doesn't work, we'll go back to the way it's been for all these years. All we're gonna do is try and see if we can make the holiday even better than the good memories we all have."

Needless to say, the shorter holiday gathering wasn't perfect. There were still a few stressful moments and one particular relative who was being difficult. But overall, Evelyn found, "It was 75 percent better than any previous holiday event. There was so much less chaos, and far fewer uncomfortable moments. All of us went home feeling close and connected instead of exhausted and resentful. My mother-in-law even got four phone calls from family members who said it was the best holiday event they can remember."

During the weeks following this holiday experiment, Evelyn found that her mother-in-law was still a little unsure of whether she wanted to commit to doing the shorter version again the next year. "She told us, 'I love the feeling of savoring a whole day spent together with the people I care about most.' I was tempted to scream at her and say, 'Can't you see how great it was this year and how awful it's been for so long?' But I knew we had sincerely meant it when we promised her that this was a one-time experiment with no obligation to make it permanent."

Evelyn thought she would have to compromise, but then something wonderful happened. "My mother-in-law usually won't take advice if it comes from me, yet she's a lot more compliant if the advice comes from my husband. So I kept my mouth shut and didn't get into a power struggle with her. But then my husband said to her, 'Mom, I got three more phone calls from relatives who say this was the most enjoyable holiday gathering we've ever had. Are you sure you want to go back next year to the seven-hour version, which had so many problems?' Hearing that from her beloved eldest son, my mother-in-law smiled and said, 'No, we don't really need to do the seven-hour version. I'll miss it, of course. But I think I'd rather see my loved ones getting along. It was so satisfying to look out across the room this year and see everyone having a good time at dinner. I'm not blind—I know it was much calmer and easier than it's been for a long, long while.'"

WAY #2: LOOK FOR A DEEPER SENSE OF CONNECTION

The feelings of frustration and alienation you may have experienced at family gatherings often happen because in most families everyone is expected to do the same thing as everyone else, as though one size fits all. For example, if your family loves to sit around a big table to argue about political topics and you don't like arguing about political topics, your chance for family closeness may have been hampered year after year by these heated arguments. Or, if your relatives tend to spend every family gathering glued to the television set watching baseball, football, basketball, car racing, or golf, and you don't enjoy watching sports, then you may feel unable to connect in a deeper way with your sports-obsessed family.

In the same way, sitting around a formal dining room table with the conversation being dominated by a few self-absorbed or highly opinionated individuals is less than pleasurable. Have you ever noticed that certain of your relatives don't seem to care a bit that they're repeating themselves and boring everyone to tears? They simply want a captive audience, and they're not really interested in what's on your mind.

Setting the Stage for Togetherness

What can you do to change these unpleasant holiday routines? What might make a family gathering more comfortable for those of you who have felt left out in the past? What can you do to make meaningful conversations more likely? Here are a few ideas for you to consider instituting at your next family gathering:

Set smaller tables. Urge the host or hostess ahead of time to put family members at a larger number of smaller tables, with less outgoing family members seated next to someone they like, so they can have more intimate conversations. Unlike a large table where one or two relatives tend to dominate, this gives everyone a chance to feel involved and included in the meal conversations.

Plan for a diversity of activities. In addition to the inevitable political conversations or the television sports-watching, make sure there are appetizers and chairs arranged for conversation circles in other parts of the house. Rather than requiring each person to do what the most dominant relatives think is important, be sure to allow for deeper conversations to develop before, during, and after the meal.

Ask ice-breaker questions. Whether you are at one large table or a series of smaller tables, start a family tradition where each person has the chance to answer a question that is designed to make each guest feel welcome and to put everyone on an equal footing. For instance, ask each relative to give an answer of one minute or less to a question such as:

–What is one thing for which you are thankful?

–Is there something that's happened in the past year or months that you've struggled with and that you've learned from?

–Can you share some recent good news?

–What is your favorite family memory from past gatherings?

–Has a relative who is no longer here taught you something useful or inspiring?

–What is your greatest hope for the coming year?

These and other probing questions can shift the conversation from boring small talk to deep and profound discussions. Just make sure the question is one that each person at the gathering, child or adult, can answer easily, and that will help each individual feel included as an equal. Plan ahead of time to have one articulate, sincere family member go first and be a role model of how to answer the question briefly and from the heart.

You may also need to appoint one respected and gracious family member to be the timekeeper. The one-minute rule need not be applied rigidly, but there still should be some way to keep long-winded relatives from commandeering the activity. Please note, however, that anyone who doesn't want to speak up can say "Pass" without criticism or mocking. This is important. Someone needs to state at the beginning of the conversation that it's fine to listen to others and feel a sense of family closeness even if you decide to remain silent.

"People Get Torn Apart at Our Family Meals"

Howard is a twenty-nine-year-old computer software designer who always felt left out at his family's holiday events. He told me during one of his first counseling sessions, "In my family, there are a number of highly educated individuals who love to do battle over politics, social issues, and current events. It's not that I dislike a good political discussion, but in my family, these political debates are more like blood sport. My uncle

Victor loves to rip to shreds anyone who disagrees with him. So does my older sister Muriel, who's a prominent attorney—when she was in high school we used to call her the Master Debater. At holiday dinners with my family, you only have two choices—keep quiet and watch someone else's point of view get torn apart by one of the more talented debaters, or else speak up and risk that *you* might become the next sacrificial offering."

When I asked Howard if there were any relatives in his family who might welcome a less argumentative and more relaxed format for holiday conversations, he told me, "Absolutely. My mom and many of my cousins hate the way people get torn apart at our family meals."

To begin to change the brutal atmosphere at these gatherings, Howard spoke with his mother and several other relatives about instituting smaller tables, diverse conversations, and more personal topics at the next holiday meal. As Howard told me later, "My uncle Victor and my older sister Muriel complained a little that people were 'wimping out' by not engaging as much in the traditional political slugfests. But what happened instead is that I got a chance to sit at a calmer table with two of my favorite cousins that I don't get to see very often. We had a great conversation about what we were each struggling with in our lives lately. I got to know these cousins so much deeper as a result. It was the most alive and connected I've ever felt at a family dinner."

WAY #3: STAY STRONG AND SELF-AFFIRMING

In some families, the previous few suggestions simply won't work. For many readers of this book, the controlling members of your family aren't going to budge on the "proper" length of the visits. They aren't going to permit smaller tables. They won't allow for warm, welcoming questions that respect the opinion of each person as an equal.

For many of my friends and counseling clients, the way to improve family gatherings is *not* by changing the external structure but rather by changing your internal reaction to established family routines. You may have to live with the fact that you don't have enough support for changing the vicious way people talk to each other in your family, or for fixing the frustrating routines that have hampered intimate conversations at holiday events and family gatherings for years.

The challenge you face at your next family event might be how to stop your own habit of losing your center, or feeling like a helpless child again with your relatives. I have found that even the most successful and intelligent men and women, when faced with certain difficult relatives, tend to revert to feeling fifteen years old. Has that ever happened to you or someone you know? You show up at a family event fully intending to be the mature, competent adult you are in most other settings. But within minutes you find yourself slipping back into feeling like a frustrated and powerless kid again. Everything your family does from that moment on makes you feel even worse. It becomes a painful downward spiral until you can't stand being around these people one minute longer. Ah, the joys of the holidays!

That's why it's extremely important to plan ahead of time and come prepared with some proven techniques for staying strong and self-affirming, even when you're surrounded by negativity at a family event. Here are a few methods that have worked wonders for many of my counseling clients. You can decide for yourself which of the following might help you feel healthier and less squashed at your next family event.

Bring an Ally

Plan ahead of time to have someone at the gathering who truly appreciates you and who knows that family events can sometimes shake us to our very core. Rehearse ahead of time with this friend or loved one what you will need if you get into a pickle with your family. What should this person do or say— or not do or say—if your relatives start to criticize you, make fun of you, order you around, or get nasty in one way or another? Do you want your supportive friend or loved one to speak up on your behalf or to remain silent? Do you want this ally to look you in the eyes for a moment and communicate nonverbally that you are a worthwhile human being who is still appreciated even though you have a difficult family? Do you want this friend or loved one to go for a walk or a drive with you? Or to join you in one of the other rooms of the house to hear your feelings about what just happened? Do you want this ally to give you suggestions, or to refrain from giving any advice? The more clear you make yourself ahead of time, the more successful you will be in staying strong and not reverting back to childhood at the actual event.

Have a Long-Distance Ally You Can Call

Sometimes it's not possible to have someone supportive at your family event, but you can still be one "lifeline" phone call away from someone who understands what you're going through. What I've found with many of my friends and counseling clients is that when things get nasty at a family event, we all need someone who can remind us lovingly and honestly, "I know you are a worthwhile human being, even if your family doesn't think so." This may sound strange, but it's quite common for even the most successful and healthy individuals of any age or degree of psychological sophistication to lose their own sense of self-worth at stressful family gatherings. If you bring a cell phone or if you know where the nearest pay phone is, you can have one or more private conversations that can help you regain your clarity of mind and your inner strength no matter what goes on with your relatives. You just need someone who can listen calmly and remind you, "Don't worry. You *will* survive your family." I've found in hundreds of cases that this "lifeline" phone call makes a huge difference in helping us bounce back from painful or frustrating moments.

Use Prayer and Guided Imagery

Many men and women find that right at the moment when your most difficult family member is saying something invasive or hurtful, it helps enormously to say a heartfelt prayer that no one else in the room can hear, such as "Please, God, help me to remember to breathe and stay strong even when I'm face to face with this person who is so challenging," or "Please give me the wisdom to know who I am in Your eyes, even when I'm face to face with someone who simply can't see or appreciate who I truly am." Or you can go the restroom and close your eyes for a moment and imagine yourself on the beach in Hawaii, or feeling strong and surrounded by people who love you and understand you. Just because you happen to be at a stressful family event where someone is saying things that are hostile or critical doesn't mean you can't travel to your spiritual center or use your imagination to visit a place where you are safe and strong.

"I Still Tend to Lose It When I'm Around My Family"

Naomi is an extremely competent and hard-working marketing executive for a major corporation. She supervises a staff of fourteen employees and makes million-dollar decisions with confidence and good sense. But as she told me when she first came in for therapy a few weeks before a large family gathering, "Whenever I am around my highly demanding mother, my extremely critical father, and my very competitive brothers and sisters, I feel like a powerless four-year-old again. I tell myself before each family event that this time I'm gonna keep my cool and not be thrown off by the things they do. But no matter what I say to myself before I walk in the door, I still tend to lose it when I'm around my family."

To help Naomi stay strong and feel good about herself, I offered her the three ideas listed above. She told me she wouldn't be able to utilize the first option of bringing an ally along because this particular family event wouldn't permit guests. As for the second option, Naomi decided to have two different "lifeline" friends ready and prepared in case she needed to call. One friend was someone whom she'd known since elementary school and who had seen with her own eyes just how difficult Naomi's relatives can be. The other friend was a colleague from work with whom Naomi had shared personal stories about both of their families. Naomi told me, "I'm pretty sure I can count on both of these friends to give me a boost of energy because they seem to understand what it's like to come from a very complicated family situation. It's a little risky, but I'm fairly confident that these two friends won't judge me for whatever painful feelings I tell them about during my struggles with my relatives."

Naomi also discussed with me ahead of time what kinds of prayer and guided imagery she didn't like as well as what kinds she did like. She told me she didn't find guided imagery helpful if it involved situations that seemed forced or untrue. For example, Naomi had once gone to a workshop where the seminar leader told everyone to close their eyes and imagine themselves hugging and going on a tropical vacation with their most difficult family member. As Naomi remarked, "The last thing I want to do is go on a tropical vacation with my most difficult relatives. I'm interested in feeling a warmth, a connection, and a shared history with my family members, but hugging them in a blissed-out way or going on a vacation is not a palatable idea, even in a guided visualization exercise."

So Naomi and I worked on her visualizing herself feeling healthy, strong, and positive even when she was sitting at a table with her mother, her father, and her siblings. Naomi practiced breathing calmly in and out while reminding herself, "These people cannot control me any longer. I can love them from a safe distance and know that on some level they love me, too." According to Naomi, "That visualization exercise also felt like a bit of a stretch, but it was a good stretch. I do want to feel some love for my family, and to know that they also love me. So it helps to picture myself feeling strong, healthy, and positive. It's like a boost to my immune system that will help me breathe and feel good about myself when I'm actually around them."

Finally, we discussed whether or not Naomi wanted to use prayer or spirituality as part of her inner work for staying centered and healthy around her relatives. Like many individuals who have positive and negative feelings about prayer and religion, Naomi told me that only if she wrote a prayer in her own words exactly the way it came from her heart would it be effective for her. She commented, "I don't feel comfortable saying prayers that are formal or stiff. If I'm gonna pray, it has to be honest and vulnerable."

So I asked her to create a passionate and honest prayer that might help her during the hard moments of her upcoming family gathering. Naomi came up with the following:

"Mysterious Source of all that is, help me, guide me, keep me strong. I need Your wisdom and Your infinite creative energy. I want to stay open to whatever moments of love are possible with these members of my family. Please help me to ignore whatever is hurtful and to connect with whatever love is hidden deep within our hearts for one another."

A few days after the family gathering, Naomi came to my office and told me what had happened. "There were several challenging moments that in the past would have wiped me out. But this time I came ready to be resilient and strong no matter what my family tossed in my lap. So, when my mother started in with one of her guilt trips about why don't I take her out to lunch more often, I visualized myself staying strong, healthy, and mature, even while sitting three feet away from her."

Naomi continued, "When my father started commenting on my failed relationships and asking invasive questions about my personal life, I listened for a few minutes until I'd had enough. Then I went and made a phone call to one of my 'lifeline' friends, who said all the right things. In the past, my father's comments could have driven down my self-worth for hours or days. But this time, with the encouraging words of my friend still very fresh in mind, I went back and had a great conversation with my dad about work, which is easier for us to discuss. And when my siblings started getting on my nerves, I took a moment to pray silently. Within seconds, I could feel a warmth and a connection to my brothers and sisters. Even though they can be a real pain at times, we do love each other underneath it all."

Like Naomi, you may need to work with a counselor or coach ahead of time to prepare the tools that can keep you strong and centered during your next family gathering. Or you might want to experiment on your own by inviting a supportive ally, having a "lifeline" partner standing by, or using prayer and guided imagery. Only you can decide what kind of preparation will help you stay resilient and healthy at your next family encounter.

WAY #4: CHANGE YOUR DEFINITIONS OF SUCCESS AND FAILURE

In certain areas of life, a zero-tolerance policy is appropriate. I remember back in 1986 when millions of schoolchildren and tens of millions of adults across America sat down in front of their television sets to watch a courageous teacher named Christa McAuliffe and her fellow astronauts launch into orbit on the *Challenger* space shuttle. It was exhilarating to listen to the countdown and see the huge rockets fire up for lift-off. Then, unexpectedly, the space shuttle blew up seventy-three seconds into the flight. Apparently all it took was one crucial mistake—an O-ring that didn't seal properly on an unusually cold day—to trigger that tragic explosion. A zero-tolerance policy toward error was essential in that situation.

But what might be an acceptable number of glitches or problems at a family gathering? What might be a tolerable number of stresses, unpleasant moments, socially inappropriate remarks, or insensitive actions? Is it zero? Or can you endure one or two irritating moments? How about five insensitive remarks or clumsy actions? What about ten?

Reframing the Problem

Quite often I hear from friends and counseling clients that they were hoping a family event would be flawless, and they were extremely disappointed when one, two, or several things went wrong. This seems to happen most when expectations are high, such as when people are planning or attending a wedding, a bar or bat mitzvah, a baby naming, a large anniversary party, or an important birthday celebration. Each minor irritation or awkward moment tends to feel like it might ruin the special event.

Over the years I have recommended to many counseling clients a radically different way of assessing the success of family gatherings. I've urged men and women who have difficult relatives to set a "budget" ahead of time in which five or ten things can go wrong at a family event and the gathering can still be considered successful and satisfying. In the psychotherapy field, this type of conscious and intentional change of perspective is called *reframing*. To see how this works, consider for a moment how much calmer and more peaceful you would feel inside if you had the following "reframed" definitions of success at a family event:

- Success is when you "budget" ahead of time to expect five or ten awkward moments with your relatives and you come away surprisingly happy when only three or four things go wrong.

- Success is when you ignore the egos in the room and you find a way to focus on the precious souls, the colorful characters, and the one or two priceless moments of connection and warmth that occur at even the most imperfect family events.

- Success is when you ignore the trivialities of a family event and you concentrate instead on getting to know at least one person in your family a little deeper.

- Success is when your children or grandchildren obtain some lasting memories of relatives who aren't going to be around much longer.

- Success is when you set an extremely small but realistic goal each year and appreciate even the slightest amount of progress.

Don't underestimate this last point. Big changes can happen through small steps.

"How Big Should We Set the Budget?"

Betty's case illustrates the kind of improvements that are likely to happen if you intentionally change your definitions of success regarding a family gathering. To understand how frustrating family events have been for Betty, you need to know a little bit about her background. Betty grew up in a highly argumentative family; her parents divorced when Betty was in eighth grade. For the next ten years, each family holiday and birthday celebration became a power struggle. Betty's mom wanted the event to be one way, while Betty's dad and stepmom wanted it to be a different way. Betty and her two siblings desperately wanted there to be some semblance of family closeness and peace, yet every year there were huge arguments and hurt feelings over the logistics of each family gathering.

Then when Betty got married and had children, she tried to create some stable family traditions, and she hoped she would never have to put her kids through a breakup. But soon after the birth of their fourth child, Betty and her husband divorced. Betty's husband admitted he had fallen in love with his administrative assistant at work. Once again, family holidays were a painful source of tension and power struggles.

As a single mom who knows the emotional cost of family friction, Betty has tried to build close family bonds between her four children. But, she explained, "Now that my kids are growing up and starting to have partners and families of their own, it's very hard to get them all together under the same roof for an important event. At birthday celebrations and holiday gatherings, lately, there's always someone missing or some dispute in the family that creates tension."

When I discussed with Betty this unusual step of setting a realistic "budget" of how many things can go wrong with an event still being considered a success, her first reaction was to laugh. "Oh, I would have to set a very high budget number, because in our family there's always a lot that goes wrong. My youngest daughter tends to call at the last minute to say she can't make the event. I get so disappointed. My two sons often are at odds with each other because of their recent business disagreements. It breaks my heart to see them fighting. My eldest daughter has an adorable but hyperactive child who often disrupts whatever is going on. And my younger son is married to an extremely self-centered woman who has absolutely no tact or gracefulness. Last year she told me to my face, 'When you're gone, I'm hoping to be the one who gets to keep your good dishes. I just thought you should know that.'"

Betty then told me she was preparing herself for the next family gathering, so I asked her, "How big should we set the budget? How many awkward or disappointing moments should we let happen before we get upset or bent out of shape?"

Based on past experience, Betty picked the number twelve. I told her, "If it gets to be more than a dozen difficult moments, then you can start to worry. But anything less than twelve will just be business as usual—a normal family gathering."

Using this realistic and somewhat ironic number to help

her keep her perspective, Betty went into the holiday dinner a lot more relaxed. As she told me the next week, "I was pleasantly surprised that only nine irritating things happened. That was three under budget, and it meant I wasn't my usual uptight, vigilant self, trying to make everything so perfect. I found I could finally sit back and enjoy having most of my family gathered together. My youngest daughter called me on the morning of the dinner to tell me she would be coming only for a brief time because she and her new boyfriend were going to a jazz club to see a performer they absolutely 'couldn't miss.' Normally that would have ruined the whole day for me, but this time I simply said to myself, 'No big deal. I'm still way under budget.'"

Betty continued, "There were also some difficult moments where my two sons were arguing. In the past, it would have upset me, but this time I knew I was still within the range of a successful event and I let them argue while I relaxed on the living room carpet and did a wonderful art project with two of my grandchildren. My eldest daughter looked at me near the end of the evening and said, 'Mom, you've been so mellow this year. Are you on Prozac or something?'"

Please note that setting a budget for staying calm even if five or ten minor irritations happen at your family event does *not* mean you will tolerate severely abusive or dangerous behaviors. You still need to set limits and stand up to relatives who cross the line of decency and respect. But if you enter a family gathering ready to stay positive and not get devastated by a few minor disruptions, you will be surprised at how many more gratifying moments you will be able to enjoy.

WAY #5: DECOMPRESS BEFORE AND AFTER EACH FAMILY EVENT

Sometimes it's not just what happens at the actual family gathering that upsets you or makes you feel drained or ill. Sometimes our lives are so pressured and hectic that we come into a family event close to the breaking point. Or we show up with our immune systems seriously compromised. Or we return to our everyday lives feeling lousy after the gathering because we didn't have enough time to unwind from the stresses and miscommunications.

Do you rush around and burn yourself out just prior to a family event and then get sick either at the event itself or soon afterward? What if instead of overloading your schedule prior to a family visit or holiday gathering you were to take a "mental health day off" to prepare for the event? What if you enjoyed a walk in nature, got a massage, took a bath, saw an acupuncturist, talked to a friend or counselor, worked out at a gym, or spent a little time writing in a journal? What if you set aside the day before and the day after a huge family gathering for preparing yourself mentally and then for recovering?

Finding Time to Unwind

I realize that most of us have hectic lives and can't easily do this. But what about a half-day, or a two-hour slot? Or what about just one hour of self-care so you can be relaxed, calm, and open at your family gathering? The payoff is worth it. I know from my own life and from what I've seen in my counseling clients that the simple act of unwinding can make a huge difference in how resilient, creative, and loving you will feel when you are around your relatives.

"A Very Short Fuse with My Relatives"

Norm is a hard-working film editor who used to feel completely stressed and on edge when he visited his difficult family for holidays, birthdays, and other events. According to Norm, "In my work on film and television projects with absurd deadlines, you have to go all out to get the job done. If it means losing sleep, that's part of the job. Or if it means twenty consecutive hours of staring at a computer screen without a break, that's to be expected. So it's no wonder that I often show up at a family bash feeling exhausted and crabby. It causes me to have a very short fuse with my relatives. But hey, they usually deserve it."

When I first asked Norm if he'd be willing to set aside a day for unwinding before and after major events with his difficult family, he looked at me with disbelief. "Are you kidding? I can't afford to skip out of work for an entire day."

So I asked him, "What about a two-hour block of time?"

Norm thought about it for a moment and replied, "I'd be willing to do a two-hour bike ride to get my tensions out before visiting my family. That's gonna have to be good enough."

In fact, for Norm the two-hour bike rides before and after his next few family events made a significant difference. "Instead of showing up overtired and crabby like usual," he said, "I felt a lot less stressed. I notice that when I take a bike ride and a quick shower, I tend to be a lot looser and much less edgy. So when I walked into my cousin's house and heard the familiar sounds of kids screaming, my uncles bickering, my dad trying to run everyone's life, and my mom criticizing my dad, I actually had a smile on my face. This is my very own whacked-out family. Within seconds, I'd said hello to one of my favorite cousins I hadn't seen for a while and I hugged my sister's two children, which is always a treat because her kids are so curious, smart, and lovable. I even felt a little sad at the end of the night when my niece and nephew came up to me in their pajamas and asked if they could sleep over at my house one of these days. I adore these two kids and I don't get to see them nearly enough."

As Norm and many others have discovered, if you prepare yourself, even a little bit, to feel healthy and relaxed prior to a family visit, it can dramatically change how you react to the predictable stressors at your family gatherings. Your relatives will still do what they've always done, but your inner strength and your resilience will help you through. Most importantly, your chances of creating good memories and satisfying moments with your loved ones will be greatly enhanced.

CHAPTER FOUR

WHAT TO DO ABOUT RELIGIOUS DISAGREEMENTS AND PRESSURES TO CONFORM

When I was fourteen years old, my mother died of cancer. A few hours after the funeral, our extended family gathered at my grandfather's house for the traditional evening prayer service that can provide comfort and strength to the grieving relatives. My beloved immigrant grandfather, with whom I was very close, announced it was time for the women to leave the living room so the men could pray in the traditional manner. Unlike my grandfather, I was raised in a liberal temple and so I blurted out, "No way. Mom was a Reform Jew and she would want the women to pray as equal participants."

My father and my older sister grabbed me, pulled me into my grandfather's bedroom, and said, "Stop it right now. You're being an obnoxious brat."

But I couldn't stop. I was fourteen. My mom had just died. At that moment I didn't want to compromise.

The argument lasted for quite a while, until my grand-

father's home-court advantage sealed the victory for the traditional men's team. It was my first introduction to the intensity and discomfort of religious squabbles in families.

Later, as a psychotherapist, I heard about many other
clashes between family members who have different spiritual
beliefs, or different ways of celebrating their shared religious
traditions. Religious disagreements are a major source of friction between even the most loving and considerate relatives,
especially today. It's a huge issue because a single American
family can have one member who is strongly religious, another who is moderately religious, another one or two who
are strongly antireligious, plus loved ones who have married
spouses from different religions or denominations. With so
much religious diversity, there are bound to be disagreements
and hurt feelings every so often.

See if any of the following questions strike a chord:

–Have you ever been on the receiving end of a "well-
  meaning" relative who couldn't stop trying to shove
  his or her religious beliefs down your throat?

–Have you had unpleasant or painful conversations with
  loved ones about your differing ideas regarding God,
  morality, Bible teachings, the state of Israel, premar-
  ital sex, abortion, whether to spank children, or other
  highly charged issues?

–Have you sometimes felt upset that one of your less-
  religious family members has been dismissive or

insulting toward your own cherished beliefs or practices?

–Have you had difficulty arranging an important event (such as a baby-naming, christening, b'rit milah, bar/bat mitzvah, wedding ceremony, divorce, remarriage, or funeral) because there were serious religious disagreements between key members of your family?

–Is it hard for the members of your family to agree on where to attend religious services?

–Have you ever had an argument in December over how to celebrate holidays that have both religious and commercial aspects?

–Have you worried that one of your children or grandchildren is being exposed to a different religious approach that you disagree with strongly, but that you have to tolerate because you don't want to offend a relative who favors this approach? Or that your children or grandchildren are *not* being exposed sufficiently to a faith or tradition that you care about deeply?

–Have you ever gotten into an argument with a family member about how to be a spiritual person, how often to attend services, or religious teachings and traditions you don't support?

–Have you been surprised when a family member you thought you knew well became noticeably different after he or she got heavily involved in an intense spir-

itual or religious group? Or has a family member
fallen under the influence of a spouse or partner who
holds religious ideas quite different from those your
family grew up with?

–Have you felt frustrated that some members of your
family consider you strange, wrong, or stubborn for
holding beliefs that are different from their beliefs?

There's something about religion and spirituality that
brings out the most opinionated, rigid, or patronizing reactions in almost everyone. For more than twenty years I've
been working as a consultant to the National Conference of
Christians and Jews (which recently changed its name to the
National Conference of Community and Justice), facilitating
dialogues between people with different religious beliefs.
These dialogues have included Jews and Christians discussing
their fears and curiosities about each other; Muslims talking
in-depth with non-Muslims; liberal Christians examining
their clashes with conservative and fundamentalist Christians;
liberal Jews resolving their tensions with traditional and Orthodox Jews; New Age seekers sharing ideas with more traditional members of organized denominations; and even
atheists and agnostics exploring their similarities and differences with believers. Each one of these dialogues was fascinating because when men and women sit down peacefully to
explore their religious and spiritual differences, amazing
breakthroughs often happen. I found that if specific ground

rules and techniques are used for discussing these volatile issues respectfully, the clashing individuals can not only stop fighting—they can also heal long-standing conflicts.

The purpose of this chapter is not to tell you or your family members what to believe or how to express your beliefs. Nor am I going to suggest that one member of your family has "good beliefs," while another has "wrong beliefs." Rather, this chapter will offer proven techniques you can use to help build bridges of communication and to break bread more comfortably with family members whose spiritual or religious ideas are in direct opposition to your own. It's not about debating who's got the inside track to holiness or the ultimate Truth; rather, it's about how to become a healthier family of diverse individuals sharing a common bond.

I need to warn you, however, that in pursuing a greater understanding and a more peaceful coexistence with family members whose religious ideas you dislike (or even detest), you will be taking a huge risk. You might risk seeing the humanity in someone whose ideas about God, morality, or spiritual practice offend you deeply. Or you might risk finding out that your own ideas for or against religion are a little bit elitist or insulting. To delve into such crucial issues as the nature of existence and the purpose of our souls is no simple matter. Yet I hope this chapter on respecting the religious diversity in our families will not only reduce the friction at your family gatherings but also help you clarify the type of human being you would like to be.

The three-step dialogue process described below is based on many years of experience in helping families and individuals work through their religious clashes to reach a higher level of connection and teamwork. I've found that these steps can be extremely effective regardless of the specific religion, degree of religious conviction, or lack of religious conviction held by your family members.

What's crucial is that you bring your honesty, your most personal beliefs, and your deepest compassion to this process. The best way to build bridges between people of differing beliefs is for each of the individuals to be truthful about his or her religious and spiritual concerns. Whether you consider yourself a strongly religious person, a somewhat spiritual but not very religious person, or a strongly nonreligious person, your genuine opinions and experiences are important in each of these three steps. I urge you to be honest with yourself in order to achieve the best results from this process.

EXPLORE YOUR OWN ATTITUDE ABOUT RELIGION

You might be surprised to find that this first dialogue step is not about the person who gets on your nerves but rather about your own possible hidden agenda and your innermost attitude toward your beliefs. Quite often when I mention that step one is to examine your own judgmental tendencies, the reaction from counseling clients and workshop participants is,

"What judgmental tendencies? I'm open-minded. The other person is the one who's judgmental."

Being Honest with Yourself

It may be true that the other person is far more judgmental, patronizing, or manipulative than you are even on your worst day, but I still must ask you to look within. Ask yourself if you have recently been in a religious dispute or power struggle with a member of your family who might be more religious or less religious than you. If so, bring that person to mind and imagine him or her preaching to you about the religious or moral issue that has the two of you at odds. Then answer honestly these questions:

–Is there something from your own past experiences or life's quest that makes it so difficult for you to stomach this other person's religious ideas?

–Do you ever secretly wish this person would just shut up and never talk to you again about his or her beliefs?

–Do you ever imagine yourself saying or doing something so convincing and inspiring to this other person that he or she looks at you and says, "You're so right and I've been so wrong!"

–Do you ever feel embarrassed or worried that this person will state out loud his or her religious beliefs and people will mistakenly think you are in agreement because you are related to this person?

My intention is not to stir up trouble or cause a fight but rather to help you recognize what kind of impatience, frustration, and judgmental tendencies we all tend to carry inside just below the surface. If we don't realize our own underlying edginess when discussing religious or spiritual issues, it will sooner or later slip out as sarcasm, condescension, arm-twisting, or other forms of disrespect. I've found from experience that it's almost impossible for two family members to work through their religious disagreements if one or both parties are pretending to be "nonjudgmental" when in fact they are seething inside.

"We're Both Very Open-Minded"

Susan and Bill's case is a good illustration of how crucial it is to identify your own judgmental feelings if you want to have a breakthrough in resolving the religious friction in your family. Please pay close attention as you read their comments to see if you can recognize how we all have somewhat hostile or condescending feelings just below the surface about certain religious groups, even if we pretend to be neutral or tolerant.

Susan and Bill have been married for twenty-four years and they have one child, a twenty-two-year-old son named Evan, who recently got engaged to a twenty-one-year-old woman named Claire. Susan, the mother of the future groom, is a longtime environmental activist who grew up in a very liberal family that belonged to the Unitarian Universalist Church. Bill, the father of the future groom, is a very committed and innovative developer of affordable low-income housing who grew up Catholic and still feels a connection to the liberal social activism of some of the Catholic priests and nuns he's known throughout his life. However, both Bill and Susan are strongly opposed to many of the conservative teachings of the Vatican.

According to Susan and Bill, they raised their son Evan to be "accepting of all religions" and to "judge no one." Yet when Susan and Bill came to see me for counseling, Bill admitted, "We're very worried about Evan's upcoming marriage. His fiancée Claire is far more religious than we were expecting. She not only refers to herself as reborn, but she says in the future she wants to raise their children with strict traditional values."

Susan commented, "I'm hoping this is just a phase Claire is going through. I can't imagine that someone who got such high SAT scores and graduated from a top college with Evan could be so old-fashioned when it comes to religion. I'm sure she's going to soften a little as she gets farther away from the influence of her parents, who are real Bible thumpers from Texas."

(For any readers who are half-asleep: If you didn't wince from Susan's word-for-word remarks about Claire, please go back and read the previous paragraph one more time.)

At this point in their counseling, I realized that Susan and Bill, like most of us, had no idea they were being judgmental or condescending toward Claire and her beliefs. Like most religiously liberal or moderate folks I've counseled over the years, Susan and Bill considered themselves "tolerant" toward all religions. Yet when I asked them directly if they would be willing to let Evan and Claire raise their children according to Claire's conservative values, Susan commented, "You know we're both very open-minded and we would try not to interfere. But frankly we'd be horrified if Claire started taking our grandkids to some backwards Sunday school."

Welcome to the complicated world of religious disagreements! As I explained to Susan and Bill, "I'm so sorry to have to be the one to say this, but you need to know that you're not sounding very open-minded. If you're going to have a healthy role to play in how Evan and Claire raise their children, you'll first need to take a hard look at how judgmental and condescending you seem to be about Claire's beliefs."

Since I, too, am liberal and have had some painful experiences with individuals who tried to force their beliefs on people I care about, I can identify with Susan and Bill's predicament. We liberals and moderates like to think of ourselves as open-minded and flexible, but if someone with a strongly fundamentalist approach starts in on us or our loved ones, we can quickly find ourselves becoming quite judgmental. It's an indication that maybe we, too, have some strong biases and rigidity on the issue of religion. If there's going to be a healthy dialogue in our families and in society as a whole, we will all have to work through our own feelings of intolerance. We might need to recognize the humanity and the complexity of those with whom we disagree strongly.

So I asked Susan and Bill, "Are you willing to look at the underlying contempt you seem to have for Claire's background and religious ideas? Are you willing to put in some effort to work toward the open-mindedness and love that will be necessary if there's going to be a positive two-way conversation with your future daughter-in-law about the religious upbringing of your grandchildren?"

I wasn't sure whether Susan and Bill were going to be offended by what I said. While I've found that some folks absolutely refuse to consider the possibility that all of us can at times be condescending or judgmental, in this case Susan and Bill were willing to reexamine their own attitudes. As Susan explained, "We love Evan enormously, and if he wants to marry Claire then we need to learn to understand who Claire is and not to treat her like an unwelcome outsider."

Bill agreed, and admitted, "I sometimes pretend I'm calm and neutral about certain religious people and groups who disagree with me about controversial issues. But to be honest, I've got a huge plug-in from my painful past experiences with family members and religious school teachers who were rigid and oppressive. I guess that plug-in reveals itself sometimes when I meet someone who in any way resembles these characters from my past. There's a part of me that gets furious because I wish everyone could see things the way I see them. I don't like to admit it, but at times I can be quite intolerant."

Now that you've seen Susan and Bill take the first step and reexamine their judgmental tendencies about religion, the decision of what to do next regarding your own situation is yours. Do you want to be like many others who pretend they have no hidden contempt for family members who hold opposing religious and moral viewpoints? Do you want to cling to the idea that you have no secret bitterness toward family members who strongly disagree with your deepest beliefs? If you are a liberal or a moderate when it comes to religion, can you honestly say you don't have some impatience and intolerance toward the conservative or traditionalist members of your family? Or if you are a conservative or devout individual, do you honestly believe you hold no bitterness inside toward liberal or secular family members who dismiss or don't understand your beliefs?

The first step in any healthy dialogue is for both sides to admit that there's some distance to travel in order to see the other person as a precious soul with complex opinions, rather than as an oppressive adversary. We need to look within and examine our own intolerance before we can communicate honestly.

It's not easy to face up to one's imperfections, but I believe most of us can do it, especially if our goal is to reach a new level of understanding and creative solution building in our families and in society.

SEEK OUT THE OTHER PERSON'S POINT OF VIEW

Now that you've spent some time looking at your underlying feelings about people who strongly disagree with you, let's take a moment to carefully sort out what the other person holds dearly. Step two is to try to see the religious dispute in your family from the other person's perspective.

Imagine that you went to sleep and woke up the next morning with the exact life history, values, and beliefs of the family member who has been getting on your nerves about religion. Imagine that you temporarily have become that person. Try to understand why he or she feels so passionately about the devoutly religious, moderately religious, or antireligious viewpoint that has been so upsetting to you in the past.

To gain important insights that might help improve the dialogue in your family, ask yourself:

-How does this person justify his religious or spiritual beliefs?

-What has this person studied, learned, or experienced that may have resulted in her holding this belief?

-To whom does this person feel loyal or connected to while holding this view?

-What positive outcome does this person think will happen if others—if you—were to hold the same view?

–What does this other person believe is the deeper issue
for which this particular religious belief or practice is
a piece of the puzzle?

Seeking to understand the perspective of another person
is not easy, but it's essential if you're going to have a successful breakthrough conversation with your family member
who holds an opposing religious (or antireligious) viewpoint.
It is a key step toward reducing friction and rebuilding the
heart connection you may have lost toward this person.

Quite often what happens at this point is that even
though you disagree with the other person about certain issues, you might be able to agree about some underlying
values you hold dear. To illustrate what I mean, imagine two
family members arguing about whether to spank a child. One
person might say it's a traditional religious teaching that to
spare the rod is to spoil the child, while the other person
might say that spankings are abusive or counterproductive. It
looks as if the two family members disagree.

But if you go deeper and look at the heartfelt values on
both sides, you may see that both family members want to
raise a healthy child who feels loved, who can live within reasonable limits, and who can display a healthy amount of self-
regulation. At that point of agreement, the two family
members can brainstorm and discuss different ways of im-
parting love and good limits to a child. Instead of arguing or

resenting each other, the two can become allies in developing healthy ways of raising responsible children.

Or if two family members are clashing about their different concepts of God or spiritual practice, they could use this bonding process to stop belittling each other's viewpoints and instead realize that both of their beliefs (or one's nonbelief) come from intelligent minds trying to make sense of one of life's great mysteries. It need not be a fight, but could be a caring conversation about how humbling and profound it is to be seeking to understand the mysterious creative force that connects all of us.

Ending a Painful Power Struggle

If you decide that you are serious about transforming a religious clash into a caring and productive conversation, you will probably be surprised at how quickly it can reduce the tension between you and the family members whose beliefs you have found so frustrating. For example, in my own family there was an ongoing power struggle about religion that caused a lot of hurt feelings. Specifically, my wife Linda and I each year would attend high holiday services at a progressive temple where she and I have been active for many years. My wife's parents, every year, were very upset because they wanted us to join them at their own, more traditional congregation, where the services are almost entirely in rapidly spoken Hebrew.

For several years my wife and I resented their "interference." Her parents were set in their ways and unwilling to let us go to our own services without bombarding us with a lot of angry comments and guilt-inducing remarks. On several occasions, the agitated phone calls and dinner table arguments with her parents were so upsetting that my wife and her mom were both brought to tears.

Then, a few years ago, my wife and I did the exercise described above. Imagining ourselves to be her parents, we asked each other, "What is the deeper reason they argue so strongly for attending their services? What positive outcome do they hope for?"

We realized that her parents see the holiday services from a very different perspective than we always did. For my wife and I, the search for a "meaningful" and "accessible" service are the top priorities. But for her parents and many other individuals, being together as a unified family is the top priority. Being in a traditional setting, where the prayer structure and melodies are consistent and familiar, is also very important to them.

As a result of taking seriously her parents' perspective, we could see that family closeness is not so terrible; in fact, it's a quite reasonable thing to want. For the first time, we could understand that my wife's parents' desire for family togetherness at the holiday and our own desire for "meaningful" worship *both* have a holiness and a beauty that need to be respected.

An internal shift was beginning to happen for both Linda and me—we no longer saw the issue as who was right and who was wrong. Both sides had a legitimate underlying value. Each year from then on, we experimented with different solutions that could incorporate both of our unique perspectives. One year we went to both our temple and her parents' congregation for different portions of the holidays. One year Linda and I took our alternative creative prayer book and read it silently during the more traditional service at my in-laws' synagogue. One year we invited my wife's parents to attend the entire service at our temple and achieved a surprisingly strong sense of family closeness in a new setting. One year my wife and I let go of our preference for an innovative service and we became fully immersed in the beauty and majesty of her parents' services. There were still some moments in which I was uncomfortable with the traditional approach, but it was a wonderfully inspiring service in many ways.

"I Also Have Felt Deeply Moved at Times"

I was thinking about the painful clashes that had happened with my wife's parents during the session in my office when Susan and Bill were anticipating the religious battles that might take place with their future daughter-in-law Claire. You will recall that my counseling clients Susan and Bill were feeling somewhat horrified at the idea of their son marrying someone whose religious beliefs were significantly different from their own. Yet a similar breakthrough happened for Susan and Bill when they experimented and imagined themselves having Claire's perspective for a moment.

As Bill explained, "It was hard at first to do the questions you gave us for homework, to imagine ourselves believing and practicing religion the way Claire does. I had grown up so alienated from formal organized religion that I had trouble putting myself in Claire's shoes. But then Susan and I decided to talk with Evan regarding what he's found so admirable and interesting about Claire's strong faith and values."

Bill continued, "We learned in just that one important phone call with Evan that Claire's passionate beliefs are a crucial part of why Evan is so attracted to her. According to Evan, 'Claire is not someone who can be conned or manipulated by whatever trend or whim happens to come along.' Evan told us how Claire is an extremely good person at her very core, and her religious involvement is an important factor in what keeps her so strong and centered."

Susan added, "I had always felt somewhat skeptical about Claire going to her Pentecostal church service where lots of people were raising their hands and saying the spirit is moving them. But then I heard Evan tell us how those Pentecostal services brought him to tears to see how much Claire loves God and wants to pour out her love and gratitude to God. Suddenly, Claire's religious intensity began to make sense to me. I also have felt deeply moved at times when I've attended a very spiritual service with passionate music. Yet I realized that for most of my life I've felt somewhat inhibited about admitting too openly or loudly that life is a miracle and that the ultimate source of life is truly magnificent. I've always practiced religion in a fairly restrained and cautious way. So for a moment, I actually felt a sense of appreciation that Claire loves life and the creative Source so much she's willing to say it out loud in a lively way. Maybe Claire's openness might open me up a bit, too."

Bill and Susan both said that they still disagree with Claire about certain political and social issues. But they admitted for the first time, "If Claire is able to transmit a joy for life and God, as well as a strong sense of compassionate values to our grandchildren, then that won't be a bad thing." For the first time since Evan met Claire, Evan's parents Susan and Bill were beginning to see Claire as a complex human being with great strengths. They were beginning to imagine a healthy dialogue instead of a heated battle or a cold war with Claire about their differing ideas on how to raise ethical children.

HONOR EACH OTHER'S SIMILARITIES AND DIFFERENCES

The third and final step of the dialogue process is the most risky and the most powerful for building bridges in your family. Step three involves sitting down for a creative brainstorming session with the family member for whom you have felt ideological contempt or religious friction. During this brainstorming session, you and the other person are to come up with one or more realistic answers to the following questions:

–Is there a book, an ongoing activity, or a one-time event that you would be willing to experience with an open heart in order to understand more deeply the path this other person is on?

–Is there a book, an ongoing activity, or a one-time event you would like the other person to experience with an open heart in order to understand more deeply the path you are on?

–Are there any activities, values, or basic principles that you and the other person *do* agree on?

–Are there activities, values, or basic principles that you and the other person absolutely *don't* agree about and that you will probably have to accept?

Agreeing to Disagree—Lovingly

Sitting down and having a calm and productive conversation with this other person about what you can do to learn more about each other might not be easy. You might require a counselor, friend, mediator, or clergy member to be there to support your efforts and to make sure you both treat each other with respect. Remember, you are not going to be converting or arm-twisting one another—your goal is simply to learn a little more about the complexity and depth of why you both hold such different viewpoints.

"It Was Like Going on a First Date"

When Bill and Susan sat down with Evan and Claire to talk about some healthy ways of bridging their differences, all four of them were nervous. Susan recalled, "It was like going on a first date with someone. I felt extremely vulnerable and uncomfortable."

But then Bill opened the discussion by saying, "Our goal is to open up a dialogue that hopefully will last for many years, no matter what kinds of tensions arise in our family. We'll always want the communication to be caring and respectful between the four of us. Even when we disagree with each other about important issues, it would be great if we could still have mutual respect for each person's beliefs."

That opening statement reduced the tension and set the tone for what turned into a fascinating brainstorming session. As a result of their initial dialogue session, Susan, Bill, Evan, and Claire came up with a creative list of possibilities for addressing the four issues listed above. Over the next few months they tested out a few of these good ideas.

Susan and Bill attended a few Sunday worship services at Claire's church. According to Bill, "I still found myself a bit reserved, but I could see that Susan was deeply moved by the sincerity of Claire's close friends at church and the energized way they celebrate life and spirituality. Susan told me at one point in the service, 'I wish I had grown up in a congregation that included this much closeness and aliveness.'"

Claire agreed to come along to an all-day workshop on

spirituality and environmental issues at Susan's Unitarian church. Claire also joined Susan at a luncheon where she met Susan's longtime minister, who is a highly regarded spokesman for many liberal causes. According to Claire, "I loved the teachings at the workshop and the opportunity to combine spirituality and care for God's creations. I must admit, though, that I didn't agree with everything the minister said at the luncheon. But I could see we come from similar places in trying to bring our love for God into the world."

Evan and Claire, for their parts, made a promise to Susan and Bill that they would always teach their future children how both sides of an issue can have an ethical and compassionate basis. They promised that even when they disagreed with Susan and Bill's position on an issue, they would expose their children to both viewpoints and treat both sides with respect. For instance, Claire told her future in-laws, "I don't think you and I will ever be in total agreement about abortion, but I will always respect the fact that your stance and my stance both come from a deeply spiritual place and that we simply have different ways of doing what we think is for the highest good. I believe it's healthy that our kids will see us model how family members can agree to disagree lovingly."

You may find that in your own family, the first dialogue session is a lot less smooth or productive than what happened for Susan and Bill. But don't give up. In each of our families, there is always the possibility that even the most rigid and dogmatic individuals will see that you are willing to respect the depth of their beliefs, even if you disagree respectfully with the conclusions they are recommending. If this family member feels understood and respected by you, there is a good chance that sooner or later this person will start to recognize that you, too, have a legitimate basis for your own beliefs and opinions.

I can't predict whether there will be a breakthrough regarding the religious warfare in your particular family. But I have seen from experience that in most cases when you use this three-step dialogue process to work through your own judgments and intolerance, amazing kinds of bridge building can occur.

Our world is currently facing a dangerously high level of disrespect and intolerance between religions and within varying denominations of each religious tradition. Our families, our schools, our neighborhoods, and our society need to find creative solutions in which strongly divergent views can coexist peacefully. How well we dialogue with our own family members is the beginning of this search for mutual respect and coexistence. Good luck!

CHAPTER FIVE

HOW TO RESOLVE FAMILY BATTLES ABOUT FOOD, WEIGHT, CLOTHES, AND APPEARANCE

One of the great ironies of life is that most people say hurtful things to their loved ones that they would never say to a stranger, or even to an enemy. To a stranger walking down the street, one would never say, "You're looking a little heavy" or "I don't think that color looks good on you." Nor would a decent person say to a stranger, "Where did you get that awful haircut?" or "Is that a cold sore you've got there on your lip?" Yet quite often you will hear family members say these and other critical or invasive things to each other, often under the guise of "I was just trying to be helpful."

If this never happens in your family, then count yourself among the lucky few. In the vast majority of families it's hard to get through a family event without one or more relatives saying something highly personal that hits home in someone's most vulnerable spot. At the supposedly happiest times of the year, tens of millions of Americans show up at family gatherings hoping to have a good time, only to find themselves amazed once again at some of the insensitive things that come out of people's mouths.

For a moment, imagine how rich you would be if you had one dollar for every time someone in the fifty United States turned to a loved one at a birthday dinner, holiday gathering, or other family event and made a questionable comment about someone's weight or appearance. Would you be as rich as Oprah Winfrey? Steven Spielberg? Bill Gates?

At your own family encounters, do you have one or more relatives who often say hurtful things under the guise of being helpful?

–"It sure looks like you've put on a few pounds."

–"Is that really what you're going to wear?"

–"Eat! Eat! Eat! I didn't cook all day for nothing."

–"Are you sure you should be eating *that*?"

–"You eat like a bird. Are you starving yourself?"

–"I see it's been a while since you had your roots done."

–"You don't look well, darling."

–"You shouldn't smile like that. It gives you wrinkles."

–"Stand up straight. You don't want to look like a loser, do you?"

–"Forget about your diet. This is a special occasion. Have some dessert."

–"That outfit makes you look like a slut."

–"Is that a blemish on your face?"

–"Oh, try some meat. You're not really a vegetarian."

–"Unfortunately, you've got your father's nose."

–"You're thin as a rail. We've got to fatten you up."

–"I saw [your old friend from way back in high school] and she looks great. Have you considered having some work done?"

What can you do—if anything—to prevent such comments from being made in the future?

If you were to confront your most difficult relative about why he is trying to hurt you with his critical remarks, he would probably look at you like you're crazy. "I'm not trying to hurt you," he is likely to say. "I'm trying to help you." Just as a parent reaches over and cuts the solid food in order to help a two-year-old eat her dinner, so do your relatives think they are doing you a favor when they comment on your appearance. The big difference is that you are no longer two years old and there's something bizarre about a relative who can't stop trying to control your eating habits, choice of clothes, and other private matters.

As a therapist who has witnessed hundreds of families in my office arguing about food, clothes, weight, and appearance, I can offer a few psychological reasons why "helpful" relatives can't seem to stop themselves from saying invasive and hurtful things to the person they think they are helping. I've found that in most cases, the person giving advice is knowingly or unknowingly trying to pass along a painful family legacy about food or appearance that has been given in the past to him or her.

What do I mean by a "painful family legacy?" For one of my counseling clients, it was simply that her overweight grandfather, who died from clogged arteries, was always saying, "*Mangia, mangia*, eat, eat!" This pressure to overeat at every meal then got passed to my client's parents, who attempted to pass on the legacy by always urging her to eat more. Even if she was absolutely full or on a diet, her relatives felt compelled to push her to "*Mangia, mangia*, eat, eat, don't stop until you can barely stand up." As this client told me during a counseling session, "I love my family, but they are so focused on eating mass quantities of food it drives me crazy."

Or, the painful family legacy might be that someone told your grandmother at least one thousand times that she should lose a few pounds. Then your grandmother told your mother at least five hundred times that *she* should lose a few pounds. In turn, your mother said to you at least three hundred times that you should lose a few pounds. This painful legacy about weight loss and never being thin enough gets passed along from one generation to the next. At every family gathering, the pressure to "lose a few pounds" becomes as crucial to the meal as a napkin or a fork.

UNDERSTANDING AND RESPONDING TO INVASIVE COMMENTS

The next time a family member gives you unsolicited advice or criticism about your weight or appearance, what will you do? Will you let it creep into your mind and make you insecure? Will you blow up in an angry outburst? Will you pretend it doesn't hurt you, when in fact it does?

To help you resolve what has been irritating you for so many years, consider the following situations to give you ideas about what you can do to respond more effectively to family pressures over such personal matters as weight and appearance. As you carefully read the following four dilemmas, notice which characters resemble the ones in your own family.

Dilemma #1: A Vain Relative Wants You to Be Looks-Obsessed

I once counseled a very handsome actor who dreaded each family gathering because his good-looking mother was endlessly critical of every minor physical imperfection the son had. According to this actor, "My mother has spent her entire life using her good looks to her advantage, so she's always in my face commenting on what I wear, telling me how to fix my imperfections, and how to associate only with certain kinds of people. It's suffocating to be monitored and criticized by her year after year. Now she's on my case trying to coax me into getting Botox shots so I won't have any wrinkles.

She's so terrified of losing her good looks, and that fear gets transferred to me whenever we're together."

If one of your own family members has a lifetime history of using her looks to get others to comply with her wishes, of course this person will want you to use the same ploys. This person feels compelled to give you endless amounts of unsolicited advice about how to look just right, dress just right, and move just right in order to win friends and influence people. Or you may have found that this person is constantly badgering you with comments about your physical imperfections, hoping to inspire you to be as vigilant about your physical state as she has been.

Because this family member worships at the altar of appearance, you probably can't stop this person from wanting to give you suggestions about your looks. But you *can* ask yourself the following question: "Do I want to be as obsessed as this family member, or do I want to calm down about my looks so that my other positive features will be noticed?"

It's difficult to change the psyche of your family members, but you can make sure that you are in charge of your own life and your own sense of self-worth. The next time you are face-to-face with a vain or looks-obsessed member of your family, you may want to say to yourself silently, "Thank goodness I don't have to spend every waking moment as self-conscious as this person. Thank goodness I'm making some progress to keep my own self-criticism in check."

Dilemma #2: A Relative Is Terrified You Might Suffer Rejection

I once counseled a highly intelligent woman whose grand-mother and mother had told her repeatedly that she needed to lose weight, change her hair, wear different clothes, and put on more makeup if she was ever going to be happy in life. Ironically, this highly intelligent woman was a basically happy person, except when she was reeling from the criticism and insecurities about weight and appearance heaped on her by her mother and grandmother.

She told me during a counseling session, "For my mother and my grandmother, there was a history of not getting accepted in the right clubs and social groups because of their plain looks. They also found it hard to land a husband, and in my mother's case to keep a husband. So they've tried to teach me over and over again that unless I do something to dramatically change my looks, my life will be compromised. I try to tune them out, but I must admit it sometimes makes me unsure of myself in social situations and sexually with my husband. My husband insists he finds me attractive, but sometimes when we're starting to get intimate I worry about whether he really would prefer someone prettier. I wish I could just relax and not be so concerned about appearance, but I still hear the warnings of my mother and my grand-mother, which make me wonder if one day I'll be sorry."

If insecurities about looks and appearance have been

programmed into your mind by insecure parents, siblings, grandparents, aunts, uncles, or cousins, I strongly urge you to consider counseling to regain a truer sense of your self-worth, your attractiveness, and your soul's purpose in life. I have found repeatedly that when men and women directly address their physical insecurities in counseling, they almost always make significant progress.

But what can you say to yourself *right now* if a family member is criticizing your appearance? As in the first dilemma, you can't stop a relative from being insecure about her looks, but you can change the way you respond to her critical remarks. Instead of believing that she is talking about you and your life, you will need to realize that most of the time when she comments about your weight or appearance she is simply venting her own inner pain. You can have empathy, but please remember that your looks and your attractiveness are an entirely different matter from hers.

The next time you hear one of your relatives trying to resolve his or her own insecurities by commenting on your appearance, you might want to say silently to yourself, "Nice try, but I'm not traveling down that negative road with you. My job is to remember I'm an attractive and worthy human being, even when I'm bombarded by this person's toxic comments."

Or you can say to yourself, "This is a test. Am I going to let this person define who I am, or am I going to recognize this person is a lot more uncomfortable with his or her looks than I'll ever be?"

Dilemma #3: An Overweight Relative Gives You Dieting Advice

At a holiday meal or birthday dinner you might hear someone with a lifelong eating compulsion or a history of failed diets making invasive remarks in order to "help" someone else at the table. The advice-giving person has an endless supply of opinions he thinks you need to hear about what to eat and what not to eat. It's as though the more he focuses on *your* eating habits, the less he has to feel inadequate or imperfect about his own.

At those moments, you may want to utilize your sense of ironic humor to say silently to yourself, "I'm so glad this person is experiencing some relief from his self-loathing. How wonderful that I can be of service. Now I just need to make sure that I don't make the same mistake and start giving advice to someone else about what they should or shouldn't eat."

You might also need to say something directly to this person to get him or her to stop focusing on you and your eating habits. One comeback line that usually works is to say in a calm voice, "You're probably right. I'm gonna think about what you've suggested. But for right now, let's talk about something else besides food and diets." Eighty percent of the time, that kind of respectful line will get you out of the situation.

Yet if your beloved relative happens to be one of the obsessive 20 percent who simply can't stop assaulting others with advice about food, you might need a stronger comeback line. You might want to say in a calm but firm voice, "I appreciate that you're trying to be helpful, but I don't want to hear one more word about food or diet." In most cases, the invasive person will back off and the meal conversation can move on to some other topic that is less stressful.

If you're concerned, however, that this second comeback line might start a nuclear war in your nuclear family, you don't need to say it. Instead, you might want to lobby ahead of time and ask one of your most respected and powerful family members to say it for you. During a phone call at least a few days before the family meal, ask one or two of your most highly regarded family members, "Would you be willing to be the co-captain of my Rapid Response Team? When Aunt Sophie starts in on what I should eat or not eat, would you be so kind as to say to her, 'That's enough. No more comments about weight or diets. This is supposed to be a joyous occasion'?"

In most cases, if you prepare ahead of time to have at least one or two family members ready to step in for you, you can stop even the most invasive relatives from ruining your meal. You'd be amazed at how just a few choice words from the right ally can stop even a stampeding rhinoceros in its tracks.

"It's Impossible to Just Enjoy a Meal"

Claudia is a recent counseling client who told me, "My family holiday dinners are a nightmare. I try not to be too hung up about my weight, but I've got one aunt who lectures about how many calories are in everything you're eating, and she preaches constantly about which foods have too much cholesterol. I've got an uncle who likes to micromanage what everyone is eating and tells us repeatedly how he lost forty pounds once on Weight Watchers. I've got a younger stepsister from my father's new family who has a perfect body and loves to berate the rest of us for having the 'lack of willpower' that she thinks is the reason why us bigger-boned women don't look like her. My father adores this flirtatious little stepsister and it drives me crazy. Every meal in our family is like a shooting gallery, with people taking potshots at one another about how we're not quite living up to our diets and food plans. It's impossible to just enjoy a meal."

When I asked Claudia if she would be willing to speak up and tell her relatives that she wanted to focus on something other than food, she started to laugh. "Oh, yeah. They would turn on me real quickly and make the rest of the meal about *my* physical imperfections."

So I asked Claudia, "Is there anyone else in your family who could be the captain of a Rapid Response Team and insist that the conversation has to stop being just about food and weight?" Claudia thought for a moment, and said, "You know who's got that kind of clout in my family? My grandfather does. And I'm his favorite."

Prior to the next family gathering, Claudia asked her grandfather if he would be willing to speak up and stop the discussion from obsessing on food and diets for the umpteenth year in a row. Her grandfather replied, "I'd love to be the one to shut them up."

A few days later, at the family gathering, Claudia was starting to eat her main course when her calorie-counting aunt began to preach—again. Within seconds, the respected grandfather tapped his spoon on a glass of wine and announced, "Excuse me, there's a new rule I'd like to propose. No more talking about diets, calories, or cholesterol. No more giving each other advice about losing weight. Let's talk about life and adventures and what's going on for each of you. Let's make this an enjoyable meal."

As Claudia described, "It was spooky—at first there was complete silence. If we couldn't obsess about food, well, then, what else was there to talk about? But then my cousin from out of town asked us to talk about what's been the most challenging and the most satisfying things in each of our lives since we were together last year. It turned into a fascinating discussion. For the first time ever, I ate a relaxed meal in the presence of my extended family."

Dilemma #4: A Relative Equates Food with Love

In nearly every family I've counseled over the years, I've noticed there is at least one person who mixes up food with love. It might be someone who perpetually cooks way too much food and feels unloved when there is some left over. Or it might be someone who gets hurt or offended if someone shows up at a family meal on a restrictive diet or on a special food program. Instead of supporting your healthy habits, this person feels neglected that you aren't wolfing down every morsel that's been lovingly cooked for you. She can't seem to understand that taking good care of yourself by not eating certain foods might be a good thing. This food-obsessed person takes it personally when you don't overeat. "You don't appreciate all I do for you," she might think or say. "You don't really love me."

If someone in your family hounds you about chowing down enough food to prove your love for her, have a heart-to-heart talk with this person. Let your insecure relative know you do love her. Explain how much you wish you could eat every delicious bite that's been lovingly prepared. Remind this person how much you appreciate all the planning, hard work, and caring that go into the entire meal. Then carefully go over with this person what you will be able to eat or not eat at the next family gathering. Treat this person like a special co-conspirator helping you on a secret mission. The mission is that you and this person are going to design a meal that combines both love and food, but *the foods you can eat.*

In fact, brainstorming ahead of time with the host or menu planner for a family gathering is crucial for anyone who has a restrictive diet, a medical need for avoiding certain foods, a vegetarian lifestyle, or food allergies that need to be taken seriously. Especially when your relatives are likely to equate uneaten food with unreturned love, you will need to address these concerns far ahead of time. By having a proactive conversation a few weeks prior to a family event, you can make sure your family gatherings and meals will not be a constant power struggle or a source of guilt feelings.

In this pre-event planning phone call or visit, simply say to your relative who wants to feel appreciated, "I know that you care about everyone's well-being, so let's work together to see what we can make or what I can bring in addition to what you're cooking for everyone else. I don't want to inconvenience you. I just want you to know how much I appreciate all the care and love you put into these events. I need you to help me by supporting the special diet I'm on." Then work together as teammates to develop a specific plan for what the other person will make that you can eat, or what you could bring so that there will be the right foods for your special diet.

In most cases, your "I need you to eat to prove your love" family member will cooperate if she or he gets treated respectfully far enough in advance of the family gathering. But in some cases, there are prickly, self-centered, or narcissistic family members who will get hurt or offended even by this kind of considerate preplanning effort. Take, for example, the following scenario.

"Would It Kill You to Just Eat What Someone Serves You?"
Barry has severe food allergies and can't eat dairy products. He also has a mother-in-law who is an amazing gourmet cook and who feels unloved and terribly hurt whenever he turns

down any of her elegant treats that almost always have rich
crème sauces or cheesy fillings. Several times at family holidays, Barry's mother-in-law has commented, "Barry, why
aren't you eating? Don't you like my cooking?" Barry tried to
explain each time that he's allergic to dairy products. Yet each
time his mother-in-law would look hurt or rejected. Barry felt
guilty for hurting his mother-in-law, and Barry's wife felt
caught in the middle.

When I explained to Barry the technique of a proactive
phone call for menu planning, he liked the idea. Barry then
called his mother-in-law and tried to discuss a sensible plan
for the next holiday gathering. He knew he didn't want to inconvenience his wife's mom. So he offered to bring a few
potluck dishes that worked with his restrictive diet.

Barry's mother-in-law was horrified. She called Barry's
wife and cried into the phone, "I don't understand why your
husband hates me so much. I try so hard to please everyone
and then he goes and slaps me in the face like this."

"What happened, Mom?" Barry's wife asked.

"Your husband wants to bring some bland tofu dish to
my holiday gathering. That would be so humiliating. Why
can't you kids be a little less selfish and just compromise once
in a while? What is it with your me-me-me generation?
Would it kill you to just eat what someone serves you?"

Barry's wife replied, "I've told you he gets severe in-
testinal flare-ups if he eats dairy products."

The mother-in-law became silent for a moment, and

then said, "You don't know how hard I try to make these dinners special. Why do you make it so difficult?"

Clearly, Barry and his wife were dealing with someone who has a serious case of mixing up food and love. Like many of our relatives who think they are being caring when they say "Eat, eat, eat," Barry's mother-in-law was far more concerned with her own fragile ego than with Barry's health or well-being.

So I suggested to Barry, "Rather than fighting with your insecure mother-in-law about food or control, offer her a chance to be the heroine of the story. What works best with a fragile or self-centered family member who feels betrayed when you stand up for your needs is to appeal to this person's shaky sense of self-worth and let her know you are not a threat. Tell her what an amazing cook she is and ask her if she'd be willing to teach the two of you to make a gourmet, exquisite dish that doesn't have any dairy products. You might want to give her a special cookbook that uses soy or rice products that you can eat safely. Let her know that you both think she's an elegant hostess and that she's the only person creative enough to make one of these recipes tasty and sophisticated."

That was the beginning of a breakthrough in Barry's struggles with his mother-in-law. As he told me a few days after the holiday gathering, "My mother-in-law, my wife, and I had a rather unique cooking session a few days before the event. My wife and I had brought a few recipes that avoided cheese, milk, and cream, but my mother-in-law was concerned that these tofu and veggie dishes were way too boring. So she gave us a lesson on how to make the taste and the presentation as elegant as the rest of her meal would be. She was so proud of herself. Not only was she finally able to get me to eat her cooking, but for the first time ever she had gotten her daughter to take a gourmet cooking lesson from her. On the night of the family gathering, the three of us were like allies or co-conspirators. We had developed in secret a creative way to make healthy food taste delicious."

Each of our families has a slightly different version of the conflict over food and appearance. As you think about your own family, remember that the goal is not to prove who's right and who's wrong about food preferences or appearance standards. Rather, the goal is to find a creative way to become allies in putting together a family event that each member can enjoy. As Barry discovered with his mother-in-law, if you let your difficult relative be the hero or heroine of the story, you will usually find that you can bring out the best in someone who for too long has been your worst adversary.

IS IT EVER APPROPRIATE FOR FAMILY MEMBERS TO GIVE ADVICE?

While I have found that the vast majority of family members do not enjoy receiving advice from one another, there are a few exceptions. I've seen instances when a family member turns to a relative and says, "I've always been impressed at how well you dress [or how good you look, wear makeup, accessorize, fix your hair, stay thin, or something similar]. Would you be willing to show me your secrets?" If that happens, feel flattered by the compliment and by all means reveal your best tips.

The Fine Art of Giving Advice

But before you rush into a situation and risk assaulting family members with unsolicited advice or criticism, please note a few essential ground rules for giving advice properly.

Don't take your own issues out on others. Before giving anyone advice, ask yourself first if you are in any way telling someone else to do what you yourself have had trouble doing. For instance, rather than blurting out, "Don't eat that rich dessert," look inside at your own struggle to refrain from high-calorie or unhealthy foods. Then wait until the other person directly asks for assistance on how to lose weight before offering him or her your "helpful" advice.

Avoid shaming anyone. When giving advice, it's best to avoid making someone's weight or appearance the topic of conversation at the family meal. Instead, make sure you talk to the person one-on-one in private and without embarrassing this individual whatsoever. In my earlier book *The Ten Challenges*, about the psychology of the Ten Commandments, I found that the original Hebrew words "Lo tirtza-akh" in the Sixth Commandment, "You shall not murder," can also mean,

"You shall not crush someone's spirit." In most spiritual and religious traditions as well as in proper etiquette, it's recommended that you must give helpful feedback one-on-one in a respectful way and never cause anyone's vulnerability to be tossed about in idle conversation, which can crush that person's spirit. Remember, the best way to help loved ones change for the better is *not* to undermine their self-confidence but to let them know you are rooting for them to follow through on their own carefully chosen goals and steps.

Focus on what someone can change and don't criticize what he cannot. Make sure any advice you offer is aimed at improving this person's changeable behaviors and avoid any attacks on his or her character or any irreversible physical or emotional traits. Before you open your mouth, ask yourself, "Am I commenting on this person's basic body type or basic personality structure, which can't be changed? Or am I commenting on a specific behavior that this person says he or she wants to change with help from the rest of us?" Most important, you need to ask yourself, "Am I building on what this person has said she wants to achieve, or am I unrealistically asking her to become an entirely different person with shaming comments like 'Why can't you be like so and so?'"

"You Know What Your Problem Is?"

Lyle's case is a good illustration of the difference between shaming, harmful advice and truly helpful advice. A thirty-year-old middle manager for a high-tech company, Lyle had been coming to therapy for a few weeks to talk about the tensions in his family, and to see if he could make the upcoming holidays more enjoyable.

According to Lyle, "In my family, people have no tact at all when it comes to commenting on your weight or your appearance. For instance, my younger brother Rick is a very talented recent graduate of an architecture school, but Rick hasn't been able to find a job yet. So last month at a family birthday dinner held at a nice restaurant, my older sister Angela told him, 'Rick, you know what your problem is? Your hair looks like shit and you dress like a 1990s grunge music fan waiting in line for Nirvana tickets. Your clothes and your hair are basically announcing to every prospective employer, Don't hire me! I'm a slacker.'"

Lyle recalled, "There was some truth in what Angela was saying, but the Olympic judges wouldn't give her high marks for presentation. You could see Rick squirming in his chair, feeling awful that he'd been very close at several interviews to getting a good architectural job, but never quite being the one selected. Then my mom started defending Rick and telling Angela that she was being rude. So of course Angela shouted, 'But can't you see he looks like a fucking loser!' Immediately, Rick stormed out of the restaurant and drove home. By the time my younger sister Wendy's birthday cake arrived, my mom was in tears and Angela was defending herself, saying, 'What? Don't look at me. He does dress like a loser. I was just trying to be helpful.'"

Does this sound at all familiar? Do you also have a family where people give each other harsh criticism or advice in public and it turns into an ugly scene? Do you have good intentions to help each other, but often end up with hurt feelings or bitter feuds?

To change the family pattern that had been causing pain for as long as Lyle could remember, we discussed the three ground rules listed above. Could Lyle talk to Rick one-on-one instead of in front of the whole family? Could Lyle make his comments in a nonshaming way? And could Lyle focus on what Rick wanted to improve about himself rather than asking him to be someone else?

Finding the right words and tone of voice to assist a family member who truly needs advice is a crucial issue in many of our families. We all want to help the people we love. But even the slightest hint of condescension or disrespect can turn your well-intentioned advice into yet another personality clash or ugly scene.

Lyle commented to me a few days before the next family gathering, "I think my brother Rick does want and need some advice about how to dress more like an architect and less like a grungy student. But how do I give him advice without pissing him off or sounding like my sister Angela?"

After a counseling session in which Lyle practiced a few ways of expressing his caring and his suggestions, here's what happened.

At the next family gathering a few days later, all of the

relatives were watching sports on television and having cock-tails. Knowing there was at least an hour until food was going to be served, Lyle invited Rick to go for a short walk and then he told him, "I think you're extremely well-qualified to land a great job in architecture. But I would love to offer you a few suggestions about how to make the interview process more successful. If I promise not to shove my values down your throat or sound at all like Angela, would you be open to brainstorming on some ways that you might increase your odds of being the strongest candidate at each of your inter-views?"

Rick looked at him for a moment and then replied, "How do I know you're not going to be a jerk like Angela?"

Lyle smiled and said, "I can't guarantee that some stupid remark won't come out of my mouth. But I promise to treat you with a helluva lot more respect than you usually get treated with in this family."

That seemed to relax Rick somewhat, and the two brothers spent a half-hour discussing how to look, how to act, and how to respond to tough questions in an interview. Lyle and Rick focused on a few specific interviewing outfits, hair styles, and tones of voice that could balance Rick's desire for informality along with a clear statement of Rick's maturity and professionalism.

Lyle told me a week later, "On our walk, this was a breakthrough because Rick finally was willing to take charge of his appearance and stop shooting himself in the foot by being too informal. But in addition, this was a breakthrough because it was the first time I can recall two people stepping outside the family craziness and instead talking to each other with real warmth and caring."

Almost six weeks after the holiday talk with Lyle, Rick received a good job offer from a highly regarded architectural firm. Rick called Lyle on the phone and said, "It was the best interview I'd ever done, in part because of your help."

As Lyle told me during his final counseling session a few weeks later, "That one conversation with Rick was still the exception. My family continues to be somewhat brutal and invasive in the way they talk about each other's weight and appearance. But this tradition-breaking talk with Rick gave me hope that in the future there will be a few more exceptions to the family rule. I'm hoping with each passing year there will be additional chances to help each other without hurting one another. Even if my family is still pretty much the same, there will be enough successes to make me know that a few of us can come through for each other in a better way."

The next time you are with your extended family, notice the way people inadvertently hurt one another with their harsh comments about food, weight, and looks. Then resolve to do whatever you can to increase, even in the smallest way, the level of respect and caring in your family. It may seem like a small shift, but it can make a huge difference.

CHAPTER SIX

WHY FAMILIES GET WEIRD ABOUT MONEY, STATUS, AND COMPETITION

(AND WHAT YOU CAN DO ABOUT IT)

Where do you fit as a member of your family? Are you the "golden one" who people look up to and consider a success? Are you the "troublemaker" or "rebel" who faces a lot of disapproval or criticism from your relatives? Are you the "underappreciated, hard-working, behind-the-scenes person" who takes care of details while others in the family get the spotlight and the praise? Are you one of the "insiders" or trusted decision makers in your extended family, or are you treated like an "outsider" or a second-class citizen who often gets left out of crucial plans or conversations?

Whether our relatives admit it or not, every family has members who rank highly and others who get ignored or overlooked. And most people don't realize just how much their place in the pecking order has to do with money, status, and other comparisons that often cause hurt feelings and tensions between relatives.

I wish this were not the case—I wish that each family member could be treated as a unique individual with equal value and worthiness. But in fact I've found that there is favoritism and unequal treatment in nearly every one of the thousands of families I've seen over the years.

Take, for example, your own family:

Is there someone in your immediate or extended family who is given more respect or clout than you think he deserves, but because he has lots of money or status the family puts him on a pedestal and usually lets him have his way?

Is there someone in your immediate or extended family who has less status or influence than you think is fair, but because she has a lack of funds the family treats her like a black sheep, a nonentity, or a disappointment?

Do you have an affluent or classy relative in whose presence you sometimes feel belittled or self-conscious? Do you compare your imperfect home, your imperfect furnishings, your imperfect car, your imperfect kids, and your imperfect career to hers?

Is there a less affluent or less successful member of your family who looks at you occasionally with envy or resentment over what you have and what he wishes he had?

Are there certain members of your family who went along obediently with the family expectations about which career or which kind of spouse to choose, while certain other family members have followed a different path that the family has trouble accepting?

Are there some members of your family who aren't on speaking terms or who are distant from others because of a financial disagreement that may go back many years (or even more than a generation)?

Does someone in your family dole out gifts, attention, financial assistance, praise, and encouragement in unequal doses—favoring certain individuals and neglecting certain others?

Does someone who is important in your family favor one family member's children or grandchildren?

This chapter is not about how to make gobs of money, or how to invest it. There are plenty of books about those topics already in bookstores. Rather, the next several pages will address a topic that causes significant amounts of emotional distance in nearly every family: how to deal with the painful comparisons your relatives may make between you and others. We will explore how to achieve balance and satisfaction in life, even if you come from a family that pressured you to pursue money and status above all else. And you'll find a few healthy ways to respond to the inevitable jealousies and rivalries that many families foster.

THE FUNNY THING ABOUT MONEY

One of the fascinating things that I've seen while counseling is that money is an equal opportunity neurosis-maker—it causes family tensions no matter how rich, poor, or middle class you grew up. For instance, I once counseled a woman who grew up extremely poor, and even though she was well-to-do for most of her life, those memories of growing up feeling inferior to her affluent cousins never left her. At the opposite extreme, I counseled a man who grew up extremely rich and spent his entire life insecure about the fact that his relatives all looked at him as less of a man than his enormously successful father and grandfather. I also counseled a woman whose parents were quite affluent, but since their assets were never liquid and these parents lived well into their nineties, this woman always felt like "a trust fund kid without any money from the trust fund."

I have counseled numerous men and women who grew up in middle-class families where there was tremendous pressure from certain relatives to "make it big" and equal amounts of pressure from other relatives to "stay

humble and don't become like the snobby rich relatives."
There are other middle-class and upper-middle-class people
I've counseled whose relatives automatically expected them
to live as well or better than previous generations did, but
because of how expensive homes and other things are
today, they feel like failures because they are having to live
in less affluent circumstances than their parents and other
relatives. Despite being well-educated and working hard at
good jobs, most middle- and upper-middle-class people
today feel stressed and unsure of whether they will ever be
able to afford the kind of lifestyle their parents told them
to expect.

Many people have mixed feelings about money and how
it affects their relationships with their families. On the one
hand, you want to have a comfortable life and make your
family proud. On the other hand, you may have picked up
the subtle message from certain relatives that if you focus too
much on success or material comforts, they will resent you or
feel alienated from you. Or you might find that your pursuit
of financial success makes you too busy to connect with
family members, who then feel slighted.

SORTING OUT WHAT YOU
CAN AND CANNOT CONTROL

If you want to do something positive about the money and
status issues in your family, you will first need to clarify what

your relatives can change and what they are unable or unwilling to change. For instance:

- You probably can't change the minds of those family
  members who have given you the subtle or not-so-
  subtle message that "I'll love you more if you follow
  the lifestyle I've already chosen for you."

- You probably can't change the fact that some of your
  relatives are so focused on status or affluence that they
  have trouble seeing the humanity, the soul, or the
  worthiness of those people who don't care as much
  about status or affluence as they do.

- You probably can't change the fact that a few of your
  relatives are so insecure, wounded, or driven to make
  up for the financial frustrations stemming from their
  childhood experiences that they have become judgmental, impatient, or overbearing toward any family
  member who doesn't share their constant drive for
  success and status.

- You probably can't change the fact that you come from
  a family that sometimes sends contradictory messages,
  such as (on the one hand) "don't be too concerned
  about money," and (on the other hand) "whatever
  you've accomplished thus far is not enough."

- You probably can't change the fact that there are members of your family who will resent you for making
  more money than them.

To accept that you probably cannot change many aspects of the money-and-status game in your family is not easy. For years you may have been hoping your relatives would become less rigid and more understanding about why you don't share their particular concerns or experiences regarding money and status. But let's face it: nearly all of our families to some extent have a bit of craziness about financial matters and what they think is "the right way to live." No matter how hard they try to deny it, you know that some of your relatives have strong opinions about what they—and what you—should value in life.

WHAT YOU *CAN* DO ABOUT MONEY AND STATUS

While there are many things that you can't change about your relatives' obsessions regarding money and status, there are some changes that you can make happen, even in the most highly status-conscious or strongly materialistic family.

Identify Pressures You Grew Up With

Most people are unaware of the subtle but painful money issues their relatives have passed on to them. As you think about the financial pressures, lifestyle pressures, and mixed messages you've received from your family, it's crucial to take charge and tell the truth about the dilemmas and insecurities that may have become part of your psyche. Only then will you be able to make healthy decisions about your own life.

"My Father Tried Real Hard to Be a Success"

For example, I once counseled a forty-six-year-old man named Dennis who was referred to me for psychotherapy to help resolve his medical problems of high blood pressure, irritable digestion, and skin flare-ups related to stress. The eldest son in a family of five grown children, Dennis told me during his first session, "I don't really think I need to see a shrink. Basically, I've got my head screwed on straight. I just work too hard and so I've got a lot of stress. But hey, who doesn't work too hard these days?"

Like most people, Dennis was unaware of how his family of origin had contributed to his high blood pressure, his digestive problems, or his skin flare-ups. In fact, like many loyal sons and daughters, Dennis felt somewhat guilty about questioning the way his parents pressured him as a child, and he was reluctant to even consider the possibility that his family was a partial cause of his stress.

Yet as we talked about his upbringing and his extended family today, an intriguing story emerged. According to Dennis, "My grandfather was a well-to-do businessman in Asia before he had to flee to America with nothing but a small suitcase and only two hundred dollars in his wallet. And when he got off the boat, the two hundred dollars were missing. My grandfather never was able to make a satisfactory living in America. He was a brilliant man but he never caught on to the way business is done here."

Dennis continued, "My father tried real hard to be a success and make up for the frustrations my grandfather had experienced. As a result, my dad worked such long hours that at the age of forty-four he died from a heart attack and my two brothers and I each went to work to support my mom and our two younger sisters."

Describing how his siblings responded to their father's death, Dennis said, "All five of us kids were raised in a household where making up for the financial hardships of the past was drilled into us. As a result, each of us has become extremely driven, very competitive, and highly accomplished in our respective fields. Each of us also has a huge problem with stress—we all work so hard that none of us has been too successful at marriage or at raising kids who don't resent us for never being around."

Dennis paused and looked at me with a knowing expression on his face. He commented, "I guess maybe there is some connection between the stressful way all of us live and the money pressures my parents and grandparents instilled in us."

If your own family of origin was anything like Dennis's family, they probably didn't mean to twist you into knots about money and security. Rather, they were probably just trying to survive and to make sure you didn't suffer the same hardships and disappointments they had faced. Yet the pressures and stresses of trying to make up for what your parents and grand-parents never quite achieved can weigh heavily on you and your loved ones. That's why it's crucial to take time to uncover exactly what was said or implied to you as a child. Only then can you begin to reclaim your life and your emotional well-being.

To help sort out the ways in which your family has influenced your feelings about money and status, ask yourself the following questions:

-What financial setbacks, daily pressures, or painful disappointments did you and your parents face when you were growing up?

-What did your family teach you was the way to succeed or be happy in life, and what did they warn you was the way to fail or end up unhappy?

-Were there innocent or harmless things you were forbidden to do because they might make your family look bad to certain relatives, to church or synagogue members, or to the surrounding community?

-Did you or your family put forth extra measures and special efforts to prove your status or worthiness?

-When you were growing up, what specific high-status individuals were your relatives trying to impress? Who were they afraid might judge them or exclude them? Who mattered most and who was less important in your immediate family, in your extended family, in your school, and in the world at large?

–Have you ever been frustrated by not being able to afford something you wanted, or wished you could be
as classy or high-status as someone in your family,
your school, or your community?

–Did you promise yourself as a child that you wouldn't
repeat some of the mistakes or imbalances you saw in
your parents' lives? What are some of those mistakes?

By talking about these issues with a counselor or friend,
or by exploring these concerns in a journal or in some letters
or e-mails to a supportive friend or relative, you will have
taken an important step toward deciding on your own adult
values and lifestyle choices. You will be bringing your inner
confusion or ambivalence about money to the surface so that
you can examine it carefully and reasonably. Most people
never take the time to uncover exactly what kinds of pressures, comparisons, and competitions their families forced
upon them, but it's crucial for helping you to stop being run
by shame and guilt, which can make you feel constantly anxious and filled with regrets.

After Dennis explored several of the questions described
above, his face grew sad and he told me, "I never realized just
how much I've been on automatic pilot trying to make up for
what my grandfather and father never were able to accomplish. My life has been severely out of balance for many years.
My wife and my kids have been sucking it up, waiting for me
to stop being such a workaholic. They've tried to tell me that

I've become way too obsessed with money and making it big and that they just want me to be healthy and live a much longer life than my father did. Yet I've been resisting their advice and actually resenting them for not being more supportive of my workaholic tendencies."

To help Dennis deal more effectively with the pressures he received from his upbringing and find ways to achieve greater balance in his life now, we brainstormed and came up with three specific things he was willing to do on a regular basis:

- First, he was willing to start each day with a brief prayer or meditation to help calm his anxious thoughts and overly ambitious priorities. Before his mind and his adrenalin started racing each morning, he would use a few moments of spiritual centering to start the day with a sense of tranquillity and balance.

- Second, he was willing to spend a few minutes before lunch and before dinner taking a short break to listen to music, go on a walk in a pretty part of town, or read a few pages of inspirational writings. Instead of feeling caught on an endless treadmill, rushing to each meal only to gobble it down, Dennis used these relaxing moments to regain control over his chronic anxiety, his stress level, and his digestive problems.

- Third, he was willing to take one day each week for enjoying pleasurable and meaningful activities with his wife and children. Like many other workaholics I've counseled, Dennis had trouble at first setting aside this time for connecting with his loved ones, but once he got into the habit of doing it he made enormous progress in growing closer to his wife and their four children.

He told me during one of his final counseling sessions, "I discovered that the best way of honoring my father and my grandfather was not to work myself into an early grave. The best way of honoring what my dad and my grandpa went through is for me to become the first one in our family to make a real connection with my wife and kids. Even if I don't make as much money each year as my workaholic siblings, at least I will have lived a meaningful life."

Please note that even though I have recommended to Dennis and to many others the importance of putting health and family as a higher priority than money or status, I am not saying that people should neglect their work or their legitimate need for financial security. Seeking balance in life does not mean becoming oblivious about financial concerns. In Dennis's case and in many other cases, the choice is not between being rich or poor. Rather, in most of our lives the choice is between overstressing ourselves in order to chase after more money and status than our parents or other relatives had, versus choosing to live each day with a little more balance and a deeper commitment to health, family, friendships, and appreciating the beauty of art, nature, spirituality, and helping others.

Only you and your loved ones know what kinds of imbalances are currently operating in your life. And only you can decide whether you want to explore the possibility of living a more balanced life than your family said was possible, while at the same time making enough money to support your commitments. Like Dennis, your goal might be to become the first branch on your family tree to achieve the emotional well-being that your parents, your grandparents, and your other relatives were unable to find.

Make Conscious Choices about Your Worthiness

Maybe your relatives don't speak openly about money or finances but instead talk about what's proper or improper, what's in good taste or bad, what's valuable or useless and a waste of time. In many families the pressure isn't exactly about money but rather about what will make your relatives proud instead of treating you with disapproval and scorn.

As a child listening to all of these opinionated stories about who has class and who doesn't, you probably sensed your family's expectations. You probably learned—too well—what kind of status, achievements, or lifestyle choices would please them and which would make you a disappointment in their eyes.

In some families the pressure to live up to your relatives' expectations about status is a question of whether the person you are dating is from a "good family" or, conversely, if he or she is "not what we had in mind for you." Or the status issue in your particular family might have been regarding your differing tastes in furniture or home decorating, whether you belong to the right clubs and organizations, whether you drive a new Lexus or a used Hyundai, or where your kids go to school.

When you fall short of expectations, your status in the eyes of certain family members can drop significantly. Then every family visit or phone call becomes another chance for your relatives to pressure you to start living up to their ideas about who they think you ought to be.

"I Feared That My Mother Would Never Again Love Me"

One of my counseling clients a few years ago was a well-mannered but somewhat unhappy thirty-eight-year-old woman named Marna whose family traces her roots back to Boston at the time of Paul Revere. According to Marna, "The word 'status' was never actually discussed openly in our family, but we knew from dozens of stories and examples our mom told us that there were things we should never do or else we were hurting my mother—deeply. I remember in high school I dated a guy from the wrong side of the tracks and my mom was so horrified it was as though I had become a prostitute, a murderer, or even worse, a Democrat."

As in most families where there is a huge emphasis on what is proper and what is not, Marna and her siblings felt a lot of shame and guilt. According to Marna, "My older sister and I tried to play by the rules, with mixed results. My older sister dumped the one guy she ever really loved in college and married instead a well-respected investment banker from a prominent family. But he turned out to be a serious alcoholic and a chronic womanizer. My own well-bred husband never actually cheated on me, but he turned out to be a cold and distant partner. Then recently my younger sister got engaged to someone whom the family viewed as unacceptable, and that started an unspoken war of nerves between her and my relatives that has soured each family gathering since. It's not something we talk about openly; it's more an expression you see on my mother's face, a tightening of her lips and a frowning eyebrow that says, 'You've really done it this time. You've ruined everything.' Or it's the way my aunt looks right through you with her bifocals on the bridge of her nose as she takes a deep breath that seems to say, 'How could you be doing this to your mother after all she's done for you?' It's a lot of pressure to keep living up to our family's expectations."

With Marna and many other counseling clients, I've found that if you clarify and make conscious choices about the many messages that you received as a child and young adult, you can dramatically improve not only your internal sense of well-being but the quality of your life. You can substantially reduce the guilt feelings.

For instance, when Marna and I discussed who her family members were trying to impress and why they were so concerned about being proper, some important break-throughs occurred. Marna recalled, "My mother was always terrified of the rigid and opinionated members of her family, especially my aunt and my grandmother, who were forever making my mother feel bad if any of us kids did anything messy, creative, spontaneous, or childlike. My mom was constantly trying to make sure we didn't make her look like a 'permissive parent,' which in our family was considered a horrible sin. And so my mom cracked down on us real hard to let us know that if we ever did anything that embarrassed her in front of my aunt or my grandmother, then we were essentially breaking her heart. That's a lot of pressure to put on a kid, and I remember crying my eyes out with guilt one time when I accidentally spilled grape juice on my aunt's expensive rug. It felt like the end of the world, and I feared that my mother would never again love me."

To help Marna break out of the shame and guilt she had been living with for most of her life, we began to explore the pros and cons of seeking status and properness. First, we looked at her unhappy marriage, which Marna admitted she had consented to in the first place to please her mother even though she herself had serious doubts. According to Marna, "My husband is a decent human being and I don't want to divorce him. But I don't know if I can live my whole life with so much 'properness' and so little warmth and affection."

Hoping to improve the marriage rather than end it, Marna and her husband, Bret, went into couples counseling to work on the unhealthy roles and lack of warmth that had been painful to Marna for several years. It took a number of months, but Marna found, "My husband Bret is still by nature a bit formal and reserved, yet he's improved a lot as a husband because of our honest conversations and creative problem solving in couples counseling. His listening skills and his ability to show empathy and caring have gotten much stronger. We've also started to address some of our sexual problems. My mother and many of our New England relatives would be horrified if they knew that Bret and I have started taking a course in Tantric breathing and lovemaking, taught by the wife of a local university professor of ancient Eastern literature. Despite the fact that Bret and I were both raised without much physical affection or hugging from our very proper families, we've warmed up our sex life quite significantly in these past few months."

In addition to taking steps to improve her marriage, Marna began to make conscious decisions about her choice of friends and activities. She explains, "My mother has a real narrow list of who's okay to hang out with and who's not our kind. For years I subconsciously went along with her values and had a very narrow social life as a result. But in the past year I've been breaking some of her rules. Every few weeks I've gone with new friends to dinner parties, cultural events, museums, films, and dance clubs in parts of the city where my mother would freak if she knew where I was. It feels like at the age of thirty-nine I'm finally starting to create my own life and make my own decisions. I was always a bit terrified that I'd do 'the wrong thing' or embarrass my mom by living a little too freely. But the fact is that my mother is uncomfortable with just about everything I do that is interesting or unusual or that brings me joy. So why bother worrying that I might offend her sense of propriety? I've begun to realize she's in charge of her life and I'm the one who's in charge of my life."

A word of warning. Marna was able to break out of her shell in a safe way and with a good sense of discretion. But in some cases when people are raised with a very strict sense of rules and guilt, they might burst out too clumsily and too impulsively as soon as the prison door is unlatched. I hope that you don't go out and do anything harmful to yourself or others in your quest to loosen the rules. Remember, the goal is to build an adult life that is healthier and more alive than your anxious, status-obsessed family members. I wish you wisdom.

Stop Competing with Your Relatives

I've found that one of the surest ways for a family to stunt someone's growth or crush someone's spirit is to constantly compare him or her to someone else in the family. You might recognize the phrases that have been tossed around in your own family that can hamper one's growth and health.

–"Why can't you be like your brother [or sister]?"

–"So-and-so has a great job. Why can't you find one?"

–"If you love your father, you'll follow in his footsteps."

–"You've got so much going for you. Why are you the only one still not married?"

–"The trouble with you is that you're always marching to your own drummer."

–"I never had this problem with any of your siblings. Why do you have to be so stubborn?"

In most families, there is at least one person who simply doesn't share the values and lifestyle decisions of the other family members. It's not about who's right or wrong but rather a question of moving beyond comparisons and competition so that each family member gets support for his or her unique journey in life.

If you happen to be the outcast in your family, the one who has a different notion of money and status than the other family members, please know that you are not alone. The majority of creative people and unconventional thinkers throughout history have also found themselves alienated or scorned by their relatives. But what can you do to stay true to your unique way of living life? Or, if you are concerned about someone else who is the black sheep or rebel in a family that simply cannot accept this person's way of life, what can be done to support this individual? How do you make sure he or she doesn't get crushed or excluded by the prevailing values and constant comparisons from judgmental relatives?

"My Family Doesn't Know What to Do with Me"

Lauren's case is a good example of someone who has been stung by too many comparisons with her relatives on the issues of money and status. Lauren is a bright and creative thirty-two-year-old woman who told me in her first counseling session, "My family doesn't know what to do with me. I'm a bundle of contradictions to them. On the one hand, I grew up with a love for Irish and Appalachian roots music, which I picked up from my maternal grandmother and which I studied in depth during college and graduate school. That kind of creative interest makes absolutely no sense to my father, who's a self-made business owner. He thinks I'm a complete fool for pursuing my passion for music history and ethnic folk cultures. My stressful financial situation is a big joke to my older brother, who's a very prominent proctologist. I'm also having trouble with the constant judgments and advice from my younger sister, who has an affluent lifestyle and who's been divorced twice already from well-to-do guys whom she decided weren't making enough money to keep her happy."

Lauren explains, "You see, our family has a lot of emotional baggage about money and status. When I was a kid, my dad struggled to make ends meet. We lived in a very small house right on the edge of a much nicer neighborhood. My brother, my sister, and I knew quite clearly that we had a lot less money than the kids at our highly competitive high school, where most of the kids had fancy cars by junior year, while my brother and I shared a beat-up old clunker my dad bought used. We also had less money and fewer things than my rich cousins, who were always going on fancy vacations. In our family, my dad and mom were extremely tight with money while his business was slowly growing. And he and my mom stayed extremely tight with money after his business started to do well when I was in college."

Lauren admits, "I wish I could just be a full-time researcher of Irish and Appalachian culture, music, storytelling, and folkways. Yet even though my family thinks I'm oblivious about money, there's also a part of me that seriously longs for financial security, a nice car that doesn't break down all the time, and some decent health insurance. I feel most at home when I'm wearing casual clothes and spending time with musicians, writers, and teachers. But there's also a part of me that wishes I could have some of the creature comforts I see my brother and sister have. They live in gorgeous homes and I've got a tiny apartment with wood planks and cinder blocks holding up all my books."

Lauren told me during one of her sessions, "I feel so split between the suburban values my entire family wishes I'd just succumb to, and my own creative process. My mom, my sister, and my girlfriends from high school all think I should find a rich partner who'll support me. My dad and my brother think I should bail on the Irish/Appalachian thing and study something lucrative—like proctology, I suppose. I feel like I'm stubbornly sticking to my rebel path, but I'm the one who's suffering because I can't afford a new transmission for my old beat-up car."

Does Lauren's case sound familiar to you? What exactly can help a creative or unconventional person to rise above the negativity and disapproval of family members? What can help this unique individual to be successful in life, even if she comes from a family that doesn't share her vision or passions?

To help Lauren work through her ambivalent feelings about money, security, and where she belongs in her family and in the world, I asked her the following questions. See what your own responses are to these same issues.

–If you miraculously were to have the most understanding and supportive family, what specific interests and journeys of yours would you want them to understand and support?

–Who might you look to—inside the family and out— for ideas and support on your unconventional path?

–If you were being advised by the best career counselors and financial advisors in the world, what strategies and steps would you put together as a way of combining your creative passions and your need to have a decent cash flow, savings, and future financial security?

–Are there any positive traits or useful insights about money or success that you've already learned? Is there some way that you can become financially secure even if your particular style for making and saving money is quite different from that of your other family members?

Asking Lauren to look beyond her family's particular quirks about money was the beginning of a breakthrough. Like most people, Lauren had limited herself to only two options: either share the family's unappealing money obsessions, or else rebel against your family entirely. A third option that most people forget to consider is, what if you incorporated the best of your family (such as your most financially savvy parent's wisdom about money) with other nonfamily role models as well as your own traits for resilience and creativity?

For several counseling sessions, Lauren and I discussed how much she had learned from watching the financial strengths and weaknesses of a variety of individuals. During one of our conversations, Lauren told me, "If I could combine my family's savvy about money with my own creative passions about music and culture, that would be an outrageous mixture. My parents and my siblings are a little too obsessed about money, but at the same time I do admire their ability to plan for the future and stick with their financial goals. Still, there are creative people I've met over the years who were also persistent and resilient no matter what kinds of difficulties came their way. I guess there's an aspect of each of these mentors and role models inside me. My job is to make sure I get all these diverse parts of myself working together in harmony."

Lauren's realization that she could stop competing against her family was the beginning of a process of redefining her own adult identity. She and I started to brainstorm about what specific things she could do to chart her own unique path separately from the skeptical and limited viewpoints of her relatives. Lauren began taking steps to boost her yearly income from several sources that stemmed from her own creative passions for music and culture. First, she landed a steady job teaching music history as well as a part-time job at a nearby recording studio mixing and arranging songs. Over the next twelve months she also began writing books and articles about some of her favorite old-time musicians, and she fulfilled a longtime dream by working as a music producer for a few compilation CDs that did fairly well commercially. Finally, she began saving ten percent of her income every month to make sure she would be able to reach her long-term financial goals.

As with many of my creative clients who felt judged or constantly put down by their relatives, Lauren began to build an adult identity that was far beyond what her family could have imagined for her. It allowed her to keep her passions alive by working intelligently at several different ways of making money from her unconventional interests. Two-and-a-half years after she first came in for counseling, Lauren told me, "I may not be as rich as my brother the doctor or as classy as my money-obsessed sister, but I love where I'm living now and I'm building a future that is both fulfilling and somewhat secure. I always thought I'd have to choose between chasing after money the way my relatives did or else being poor on my lonely creative path. But right now I'm making a good living doing what I care about most in the world. I'm teaching, arranging, writing, and producing music. My family still isn't sure what to make of me, but I'm very fortunate. I'm living an authentic life."

To move beyond the comparisons and competitions is not easy. But if you take some time to explore the strengths and weaknesses of each of your mentors, role models, and most significant relatives, you will find yourself a little less susceptible to your family's narrow-minded judgments, criticisms, and pressures. Most of our family members were too busy dealing with survival, upward mobility, or their fragile egos to have modeled for us how to live a life of health and balance. The techniques and questions described in this chapter are not to blame or resent your relatives for how they dealt with money or status. Rather, the purpose of these guidelines is to dig deeply inside yourself and discover what you want your own life to be about, to find creative ways to build a life of meaning, purpose, and stability. Only then will you have overcome the pressures of your family.

Do Your Part to Eliminate Family Favoritism

Now we come to the final step that can change, at least slightly, the way your family deals with money and status. I call it the Fairness Coalition. Here's how it works:

- Stop for a moment and think back to a time when a member of your family (including yourself) was treated badly by relatives who kept him out of the loop, or when a crucial decision was made without including each of the people who should have been included. Or recall a time when someone was treated disrespectfully by your relatives because he or she has less education, money, or status than some of the other family members.

- Recall when someone in your family has given an unequal amount of attention, love, financial assistance, or emotional support to one family member, often at the expense of another family member; for example, when one sibling was treated better than another sibling, or, with grandchildren, when one set received more than another.

- Now consider what if your favorites-playing relative had been called or visited immediately by two or more people and told, "We don't agree with how this was handled. We need to come up with a more equitable solution." What might have happened if the unfairness had been addressed quickly by two or more family members speaking up in a respectful way?

Most people are uncomfortable with confrontation and reluctant to challenge the status quo in their families. Yet I have seen repeatedly that if you plan ahead of time, you can set up a calm but powerful Fairness Coalition that can get wonderful things accomplished with a minimum of divisiveness or conflict.

Before the next incident or crisis, spend a few minutes calling or visiting two or more members of your extended family who share your concerns about the unequal treatment that has been going on for years. Ask these sane and compassionate relatives, "Are you interested in working as a team to improve how our family deals with issues of money, fairness, and equality?" Then brainstorm together about what each of you will do and say the next time there is another example of favoritism by one of your relatives. Decide ahead of time which of you is the right person to talk to this particular relative calmly and in private to say, "We need your help on an important matter. We're concerned about a situation that is hurting some members of our family. We want to work with you to come up with a solution."

Please notice that the wording I've described above is neither disrespectful nor explosive. If two or more people talk to a family member who has been guilty of favoritism in this way, it is far more likely that he or she will consider your point of view.

When an incident does occur in the future, you can activate the Fairness Coalition quickly with just a few phone calls or e-mails. Within minutes or hours, the family member who is being unfair will have heard from two or more people who are asking him or her to do the right thing. If a stubborn or arrogant family member refuses to budge or insists that he or she has the right to play favorites or to act unfairly, the Coalition can turn up the heat on this person. You can bring in a third or a fourth family member, or your minister, priest, rabbi, therapist, financial advisor, lawyer, or family friend to talk sense to your stubborn relative. In some families it took several Fairness Coalition members threatening to not show up at the next family event or to cut back on their frequency of contact toward a stubborn relative before that relative agreed to be more equitable and fair.

I'm not recommending an ugly war of words but rather a calm, firm conversation that says, "We have several people who care about you and who care about the family. And we are each in agreement that for the sake of family harmony you need to loosen up a bit here. We don't want to pull away from you because we care about you. But if you don't start treating [so-and-so] more fairly, it's going to be hard for each of us to be as supportive and attentive to you as we've been."

"We Need to Be Unified as a Family"

Doreen's case is a good example of how to deal with unequal treatment and financial favoritism in an extended family. Doreen is an unmarried woman in her early forties whose widowed grandmother and financially savvy parents helped her three other siblings with financial support at important moments in their lives. According to Doreen, "My older sister, Gwen, got help from my grandmother when Gwen got married and needed a down payment for a new home. My younger brother, Bruce, got help from both my grandmother and my parents when he started his own business seven years ago. And my younger sister, Helen, just got a huge wedding thrown for her by my parents. I have no idea how much it cost, but the lavish seafood appetizers and the huge dry ice sculptures were not what you would call understated."

So when Doreen saved up her money from her job as a legal secretary and tried to buy her first condominium, she went to her parents and her grandmother to see if they would help her, too, with a portion of the down payment. She was disappointed but not surprised when her immigrant grandmother told her, "I don't feel right about giving you money right now. Maybe when you finally get married I'll be able to give you a little something."

Then Doreen spoke to her parents and was told, "We'll help with a portion of the down payment, but we'll need to put our names on the title document as owners."

Doreen asked, "Why? You didn't feel the need to claim ownership when you and Grandma helped Gwen buy her first home or when you gifted Bruce to start his business. Is this because I'm the only one in the family who's still not married?"

Doreen's parents looked at her impatiently and with some irritation. "This is just business," they said. "We'll help you get a place to live but we need to protect our investment and be on the title."

When Doreen came to my office and told me this, you could see the hurt in her eyes. "How could they be so insensitive? It's so clearly unfair. I've worked fourteen years at the same job and been very reliable. Yes, I'm not married with 2.5 kids, but for crying out loud, I'm in my forties and I'm not a flake who's going to piss away their money. Why do they treat their married children one way and their unmarried daughter another way? It's sick!"

For the next several counseling sessions we explored the emotional pain that this and other incidents have caused Doreen. Yet we also moved forward and put together a Fairness Coalition in Doreen's extended family. She called two of her aunts as well as a powerful uncle, and also had lunch with each of her three siblings.

Like many people who have tried this approach, Doreen found that "Not everyone was in agreement, and a few people simply didn't have the guts to speak up on my behalf. But I did manage to put together a pretty good Coalition of influential relatives. My powerful uncle, who has always been a fun conversationalist with me at family gatherings, was quite horrified that my parents were doing this. He and one of my aunts promised me they would take my parents out to dinner in a few days and read them the riot act. My older sister, Gwen, has never been able to stand up to my parents, and so she told me when I called her, 'Look, Doreen, I agree with you in principle. But I think it's wrong to upset Mom and Dad with this. Can't you just wait until you have a little more of your own money saved up for the down payment?' That's just who Gwen is and I don't know if she'll ever be different."

Doreen added, however, "I did get a good response from my older brother and my younger sister. They both admitted, 'It's not easy going up against Mom and Dad when they get rigid about something. But this is so divisive and unnecessary. We need to be unified as a family and not let our parents split us apart over financial matters. Yes, it's their money and their decision, but it's also important that their kids not be divided by resentments or bitterness that could easily be prevented.'"

It took a lot of persuasion from the aunts, the siblings, and the uncle before Doreen's parents understood that this was not "just business." As Doreen's father explained to her ten days later when he handed her the check for a portion of the down payment, "Please don't think we're bad people or that we don't love you a lot, because we do think the world of you. But your mom and I both grew up without a lot of money, and we also grew up at a time when parents simply didn't want to encourage or reward their kids for staying single. Of course we want to help you be happy in life, and frankly we wish you would find happiness with a husband. But your brother, your sister, your aunts, and your uncle each made a strong case that this is not the right time to be pushing you about marriage. They convinced us that this is a pivotal situation when the family is either going to stay unified or else be split apart. And since we don't want a rift in the family, we hope you'll understand that this wasn't easy for us, but we do want to be fair and decent."

Doreen had tears in her eyes as she thanked her parents. She told me later, "I could see this was very hard for them. They don't like letting go of this much control, especially regarding money. I don't need my mom and dad to be perfect. God knows they've got their issues and their imperfections. But I was glad this thing forced them to realize that you can't keep treating three of your children to lavish gifts and the other kid with constant pressure to be different from who she is. I'm glad there were members of the family who were willing to speak up for fairness."

In your own family, there may be some relatives who choose not to participate in a Fairness Coalition, either because they don't agree with your reasoning or they don't have the willingness to speak up to the most powerful members of the family. That's their right and their decision. But if you reach out to several possible candidates in your extended family as well as the clergy, therapists, financial advisors, and family friends whom your difficult relative respects, you will eventually have the makings of a strong coalition of men and women who care about fairness, and who care about you. Then you will have the tools to improve the level of mutual respect and equal treatment in your family. Good luck!

CHAPTER SEVEN

HOW TO DEAL WITH DRUGS, ALCOHOL, AND OTHER ADDICTIONS IN YOUR FAMILY

When I was twelve years old I saw on late-night television a black-and-white version of the classic film *Dr. Jekyll and Mr. Hyde*, based on the famous story by Robert Louis Stevenson about a dignified and articulate British gentleman who unleashes his uninhibited, aggressive, guilt-free alter ego each time he sips a powerful cocktail of mood-altering chemicals. One minute the well-educated Dr. Jekyll appears to be kind and considerate; the next, after he ingests the mysterious potion, his personality changes dramatically, revealing the selfish and uncaring Mr. Hyde.

That film has always stayed with me as a metaphor for what happens when a family member has a problem with alcohol, drugs, gambling, or some other addiction. One minute this beloved relative can be delightful and charming, but when he or she has had "one too many," a very different and unpleasant subpersonality emerges, and the rest of the family is stuck having to deal with this person's boorish behavior.

According to the most recent statistics, there are over 11 million men and 5 million women in the United States who are clinically diagnosed as alcohol-dependent or who abuse alcohol every so often. In addition, there are tens of millions of other men and women who get hostile, domineering, talkative, or edgy when they have more to drink than they should. Since most of these 30 million to 40 million problem drinkers have at least a few family members who find themselves on the receiving end of this person's alcohol-related unpleasantness, we're talking about a lot of uncomfortable moments across America.

According to government statistics, there are also a large number of us who have to deal with a family member who has a drug problem. Specifically, there are around 7 million women and 9 million men who use illegal drugs, as well as several million adults who experience serious side effects from the overuse of painkillers, sedatives, and other prescription drugs.

If someone in your family has a problem with alcohol, drugs, gambling, or another addiction, you may have experienced one or more of the following situations.

- Pretending your relative isn't acting strangely when you know that he is at it again
- Feeling like a gullible fool each time this person gets you to trust that she will be more considerate but then begins sneaking or scheming once again
- Acting like a vigilant detective, trying to figure out the

lies, deceptions, and evasive comments that this person has told you in an effort to mislead you about his problem

- Wondering if the situation would be better if only you knew the right thing to do or say

- Getting hooked into helping your relative hide the problem from others in the family, or from neighbors, bosses, friends, or colleagues

- Asking your family member before a family gathering, "Could you please not indulge this time?" and getting an angry response that says or implies, "Mind your own business"

- Repeatedly asking this person to seek help so that his addiction doesn't continue to add to your family tensions

- Screaming at this person that you can't continue to live like this, yet finding yourself unable to stick with your threats or to get much distance from the twists and turns of this person's life

FACING THE TRUTH ABOUT ADDICTION

If a relative's dependence on alcohol, drugs, gambling, or other addictions were easy to change, I wouldn't need to write this chapter and you wouldn't need to read it. But if you listen to the heartfelt accounts of decent men and women who have gotten a little too chummy with addictive habits, you will recognize how hard it is to break free once you are hooked. Here are a few examples of what I've heard in my office. See if any of these stories sound familiar to you.

> I have one counseling client who continues to insist that he is not a problem drinker, even though his wife and kids have told me on several occasions that whenever he's had two or more glasses of wine, they notice that the caring and considerate father and husband they love tends to disappear for a couple of hours, replaced by an edgy, impatient, controlling—well, Mr. Hyde. "He'll often say or do something that causes our dinner guests to wonder why we put up with his ugly behavior. But if we mention it to him, he'll laugh and say, 'You are so wrong. I barely even had any wine. It takes a lot more than that before I've had too much.'"

> Recently I counseled a man who told me, "I used to do a few hits of marijuana only on special occasions—to celebrate some success or to pick me up when I'm having an especially hard day. But now I'm craving a few joints even when there's nothing much to celebrate or no horrific crisis to resolve. I just like the familiar feeling of the paper in between my fingers, lighting up, and pulling in that bittersweet smoky escape from my life. Lately I'll

use any excuse to sneak out behind the garage and take a few puffs. It's heaven and I don't really care if my wife doesn't approve."

A few years ago I counseled a woman who had lost two jobs, suffered the breakup of a great relationship, filed for bankruptcy, and alienated her two adult children because of her recurring addiction to gambling. Yet this intelligent woman looked me right in the eyes and said, "I have my gambling under control; I always know when to get out. I just do it because it's enjoyable. The sounds and the smells inside the casino are deliciously tacky. When I'm picking the right numbers and the winnings are piling up in front of me, all time stops and I'm completely at peace for a few moments. What's so bad about being at peace, surrounded by a crowd of new acquaintances all having fun and feeling alive?"

Many years ago I counseled a woman who was very successful at her prestigious, high-pressure job, and quite charming to talk with, but she admitted during one of our sessions, "I'm outwardly strong but so terrified inside most of the time. The one relief I get is when I pour myself a good stiff martini. Watching the liquid swirl around, hearing the clink of the ice cube against the glass, and then bringing it up to my lips—the whole ritual is like being with

an exquisite lover who makes me feel relaxed, secure, and completely protected. I have been in a
love affair with these delicious martinis ever since
the first time they helped me blot out all my insecure thoughts and feelings. My business associates
and my boyfriend have begged me to stop because
they say it makes me kinda spacey and forgetful,
but no one in my life realizes just how much I need
this daily dose of relief that always takes the edge
off no matter how much pressure I'm under."

The Light Bulb Has to Really Want to Change

When I hear stories like the four listed above from people
who are strongly attracted to alcohol, drugs, or gambling—
and believe me, I hear many—I often think of the old light
bulb joke regarding psychotherapy. In case you haven't heard
it, it goes as follows:

Question: How many therapists does it take to change a
light bulb?

Answer: The light bulb has to really want to change.

It doesn't matter how much you want your family
member to recover, improve, change, or grow. What matters
is the motivation and persistence of your troubled relative. His
desire for change is the most important ingredient that deter-
mines whether or not he is going to get better any time soon.

The good news is that some of our family members *are*
motivated to change; they just need some help from nonjudg-

mental but honest family members to make sure they stay on track with their goals of improvement. The bad news is that most *aren't* sufficiently motivated, and no amount of badgering, coaxing, confronting, or manipulating is going to help.

Can our own loved ones break free of their compulsions? Can we ever be free of the difficult behavior related to their dependency? Can therapy or rehabilitation programs help? Can books, tapes, or medication make a difference? To determine all this, think about your relative's true degree of motivation. Would you call this family member extremely motivated to change this habit? Or would you say this person is a little motivated but easily thrown off track? Or would you have to admit that your family member is seriously resistant or reluctant to such change, despite how much the rest of you have been trying to convince this person of the need for change?

This kind of honesty is important because if you keep pretending your family member is more motivated than he or she truly is, then you are also living in that highly populated State of Denial. Breaking out of denial and admitting the truth about your family member is the first step toward reclaiming your own sanity and freedom.

STRATEGIES FOR DEALING WITH AN ADDICTED FAMILY MEMBER

If you want to save yourself and your nonaddicted family members a lot of wasted effort and ugly power struggles, here are three things you can do to be more effective in responding to a troubled or addicted family member. None of these strategies is guaranteed or invincible, but I have seen them lead to significant improvements in the majority of families who tried them. If you want to create a little more serenity and a lot less frustration in your family, consider doing one or more of the following.

Discuss How This Person's Behavior Is Affecting the Family

In most families there is a lot of tiptoeing around alcohol, drug, gambling, or other addiction problems. To break out of this dishonesty, invite each member of the family to a brainstorming session to consider the following questions:

–What are the concerns you have about bringing outsiders to family events in light of your family member's unpleasant behaviors?

–When have you felt personally attacked, ignored, mistreated, or let down by the family member who has been engaging in addictive habits?

–What have you been saying to yourself to excuse this person or to deny that it's affecting your life?

–What have you begun to do to compensate or cover for this person?

–What do you imagine your family interactions could be

like if this person were to get help and change his or her unpleasant behavior?

–In what ways has this person's difficult behaviors caused you to become less trusting or more walled off from other people in your life?

–Has the chaos generated by this troubled person caused you to be sidetracked or too distracted to give your best energy to some creative project or important relationship?

These concerns are to be written down and then spoken aloud without attacking the addicted person's character or underlying goodness. We're talking here about problem behaviors and not about someone's soul or worthiness as a person. But we do need to get each family member's reactions out on the table so we can assess the full impact of the addicted person's behavior.

In some families, where the troubled individual is a caring and nondefensive person, this fact-finding discussion about the impact on the family can take place with the addicted person present. In other cases, where the addicted person is too fragile, too defensive, or too explosive to be included in the initial discussion, the family should meet first without him or her there.

In either case, the goal of this meeting is not to trash the troubled individual who has an addiction problem, but rather to assess how the addiction is influencing each of the other family members. For as long as the family is locked in silence or denial regarding the elephant in the room that no one is allowed to mention, healing and change will be blocked.

"She Had No Idea How We All Felt"

Edward's situation is a good example of what can happen when there's a family meeting to bring together everyone's different insights and reactions about an addicted family member. Edward came to one of my workshops at UCLA Extension on "Dealing with Difficult Family Members." Afterwards he told me that he is a fifty-six-year-old accountant whose fifty-nine-year-old sister, Sheila, is a divorced nurse with two grown children. Sheila suffered a serious back injury several years ago and started taking prescription medication for sleep inducement and pain reduction.

According to Edward, "My sister became a little too fond of her medication and it eventually got to the point where she was becoming addicted. She started to lose her memory somewhat, she became extremely moody at times, and she was acting in unusual ways because of the side effects from the pills. My other two siblings and I were quite worried about Sheila. We'd heard rumors that she was starting to act unprofessionally at work, and she'd broken up with her most recent boyfriend, who told us he was tired of living with her constant mood swings ever since she'd been popping so many pills each day."

In phone calls and at family gatherings, Edward and his siblings tried to reason with Sheila that, like millions of others, she had become addicted and needed to seek help. But Sheila laughed at their suggestion, saying, "You guys don't know anything. I've got this under control. After all, I'm a nurse and you don't have any experience with this except the nonsense you read on the Internet."

Then a few months later Sheila nearly died in a car crash that happened because she fell asleep at the wheel. Edward thought the car accident would make an impact on Sheila. But like many people who have a fondness for a particular addictive substance, Sheila came out of the hospital with an even stronger desire to keep herself medicated with higher doses of painkillers than her doctor had prescribed. Using her connections as a nurse, Sheila managed to coax a few doctors to write up an extra supply of each of her favorite pills.

A few weeks after Sheila was released from the hospital, Edward called each of his siblings and they decided to schedule a family meeting the next Sunday that would include Sheila, all her siblings, Sheila's two adult children, and Sheila's work friend Josie, a nurse who had battled a similar type of addiction to pain medication several years earlier. When Edward first asked Sheila to attend, Sheila was somewhat hesitant, saying, "You're wasting your time. I've got this under control." But when Edward said to her, "Hey, Sheila, you're a nurse. You should be there Sunday. You can explain to us exactly what you're taking and why we should stop worrying. And you can listen while we each tell you what it's been like for us these past few months watching someone we love in so much distress. I think we all need to have this kind of an open and honest conversation. What do you say?" Sheila paused for a moment and then said, "Fine. I'll be there. Someone's got to make sure you get the facts straight."

Prior to the meeting, Edward did two things that I recommended to him to help make the family discussion more successful. First, he reminded each of the nonaddicted family members and friends that they should be honest about their concerns but not attack Sheila or criticize her. While many years ago it was fashionable for "family interventions" to sometimes turn into a verbally brutal attack-fest in which all the relatives ganged up on an addicted family member and then forced that person into a recovery program, in recent years it has been found that this type of brutality is unnecessary in most cases. Compassionately telling your troubled family member how much you care about him or her and how frustrating it is to have your life turned upside down by this person's refusal to seek help is usually enough to spur a somewhat-motivated family member into treatment.

Second, Edward reminded Sheila several times during the days leading up to the family meeting that "Each of us still loves you, Sheila, and we always will. We all know you are a good mom, a great sister, an excellent nurse, and a good friend. This meeting is to figure out if the side effects of the medication are changing your behavior in ways that would happen to any of us if we were in the same painful situation you've been in. It's not about judging you. It's about hearing your ideas on what the medication is or isn't doing, and about what each of us has experienced these past few months. It's a chance for all of us to share information without attacking or criticizing one another." This type of clarification of the purpose of a family meeting is crucial. It lets your troubled loved one know that he or she is still a respected and worthy human being, even if his or her addictive behavior has been getting on people's nerves.

The family meeting on Sunday afternoon started out rather awkwardly when Sheila spoke up first and announced, "I just want you guys to know I appreciate your concern but I'm fine and I don't need any help." As Edward told me a few days later, "I believed at that moment this was going to be a huge fiasco. My know-it-all sister Sheila was not going to listen."

Yet after each of the gathered relatives and friends had spoken honestly and lovingly about how much things had changed as a result of the medication problems, Sheila's eyes filled with tears. She told them, "This is very hard to hear. I never thought my little problem was causing so much discomfort to those who mean so much to me."

Edward told me several weeks later, "That meeting was the first of several key moments in Sheila's recovery. She had been tuning us out for several months and she had no idea how we all felt until we sat down and finally got her to take us seriously. That meeting led to Sheila joining a twelve-step program that specializes in prescription drug addictions. She began going to meetings, talking at least once a day with her sponsor, and reading up on the recovery stories of men and women whose behavior, moods, and memory had been temporarily impacted by pain medications and sleeping pills. It's been hard work, but Sheila's made a lot of progress getting the drugs out of her system and repairing the damage they did to her work, her personal life, and her family relationships."

Don't Get into a Power Struggle

Not everyone has the kind of satisfying breakthrough that occurred for Edward and his sister Sheila. Sometimes the caring family members are less able to bring about positive change. As I mentioned earlier, sometimes the addicted family member is too fragile, too defensive, or too explosive to be able to attend a family meeting. So you need to know about the other options that might help and, above all, how to avoid making things worse.

"I Wanna Kill the S.O.B."

Gerard is a thirty-four-year-old film editor whose father-in-law, Merv, a successful businessman in his sixties, came to my office to seek help. According to Merv, "My son-in-law Gerard is in trouble and he just refuses to deal with it. We knew when my daughter Julianne met Gerard six years ago that he was a bit of a drinker, but we had no idea the problems this would cause. In the past few months Gerard has been drinking a lot more than we'd realized. A few weeks ago he lost an important customer after getting tipsy and way too talkative at an important industry fund-raiser. Then Gerard smashed up his new car by driving home drunk and plowing it through the interior wall of the garage. Last week my daughter finally told us that Gerard's been having several glasses of wine each night before dinner and screaming at their two young toddlers whenever the kids misbehave in even the most normal ways. Frankly, I'm worried about my daughter and I'm worried about our grandchildren."

A week before Merv called me, he had tried on his own to set up a family intervention to confront Gerard about his drinking problem. It backfired. Merv's daughter Julianne got upset during a phone call a few days before the scheduled intervention and accused her parents of trying to undermine her marriage. Gerard heard about the proposed intervention and told his wife that she was to stop calling or visiting her parents until they apologized to him personally. Merv's wife, Gladys, was thinking about calling Child Protective Services to come and investigate whether the two young children were safe living with an explosive drinker; Merv and his wife were debating day and night about whether or not to call for help. As you often find in families where there is an addicted individual, everyone was feeling agitated and upset.

During our initial conversation I tried to support Merv's frustration at feeling powerless to help his daughter get her husband into treatment. Like most family members of an addicted person, Merv was feeling a justified fear that his daughter and her kids were heading for a long bout of chaos and unpleasantness.

But I also noticed that Merv had only harsh things to say about his son-in-law, and he seemed determined to use the recent drinking incidents as a justification for telling Julianne her marriage was over. Merv told me, "I am not going to let my only daughter ruin her life by staying married to this bastard. She deserves so much better than this."

I told Merv his feelings were understandable. It's very painful to be a parent and watch your grown children make decisions you disagree with. But I also asked him, "Do you know why your daughter married Gerard? Is there a good side to him that she's still in love with?"

Merv answered quickly, "I haven't the slightest clue."

Then I asked him, "Would you be willing to talk to her calmly and hear her side of the story?"

Merv replied in an instant, "What would be the point? The guy is a complete loser. Sure he makes a decent salary, but it's just a matter of time before he ruins that, too."

My goal at this point in the counseling session was to help Merv see that he was reducing his chances of being effective by remaining so closed-minded and controlling. It's a normal human reaction to want to jump in and fix or give orders to a troubled family member. But it usually tends to make things worse.

I said to Merv in a calm voice, "Do you realize that you sound not at all interested in your daughter's side of the story? I know you love her, but would you be willing to hear the reasons why she married Gerard and why she's hoping to stay in the marriage?"

Merv looked at me with a sour expression on his face that appeared almost as if he had bitten into a piece of tinfoil. I doubted he was feeling overjoyed at this moment that he had come in for counseling.

I looked at him as he sneered silently at me and I said, "My guess is that you are a person who doesn't like being told what to do."

"Damn straight," he replied.

"Well, neither does your daughter and neither does your son-in-law. If you want to be effective with them, you're gonna need to start listening and stop giving orders."

Merv commented, "That's not gonna be easy, especially since I wanna kill the S.O.B."

I smiled and said, "Nope, it's not gonna be easy. But do you think you can start listening and stop giving orders?"

Merv puffed out his chest and said, "I can do anything if I try hard enough."

That was the beginning of a breakthrough for Merv and his family. Like many intelligent and successful people, Merv had felt furious that an addiction was creating such havoc in his life. Yet as they teach in Al-Anon and other programs for helping family members cope with an addicted or troubled family member, "The sooner you stop trying to rush in and control everything and everyone, the sooner things can begin to change."

The next week, Merv and his daughter Julianne met for lunch. Merv began by apologizing and said, "I've been seeing a counselor to talk about what's been going on in our family. I've been told that I've been acting somewhat bossy and disrespectful toward you and your marriage. The counselor said I've never really stopped to consider your feelings about why you fell in love with Gerard and why you're working so hard to keep the marriage going. Is that correct?"

Julianne grinned and took her father's hand, "Oh, Dad, you're something else. I never thought I'd see the day when you'd apologize for being bossy or you'd ask to hear my feelings about something you'd already made up your mind about."

Then she went on to describe what a passionate, intelligent, and kind-hearted person Gerard can be when he's not drinking, and what a great father he is with their kids when he's sober. She had tears in her eyes as she said, "I still love my husband but I'm worried about him. Gerard's mom had a drinking problem and she was also diagnosed as manic-depressive, or bipolar. I'm hoping Gerard will get help, but there are two obstacles we've got to overcome. First of all, Gerard won't go to Alcoholics Anonymous because he's totally opposed to the 'higher power' language they use. I'm a spiritual person and I love the support I've gotten at Al-Anon these past few months. But Gerard flips out when they talk about turning things over to God."

Julianne continued, "The second obstacle is that Gerard won't stop drinking long enough to see if any of the bipolar medications will help him. We've been told by our internist that many people are like Gerard—using an ineffective medication such as alcohol to self-medicate a serious illness like depression or mood swings. But the effective medications, such as lithium, Depakote, and Tegretol, don't work very well if there's alcohol messing things up in your biochemistry. I think Gerard understands the problem but he's having trouble accepting the notion that his drinking is an inefficient way of dealing with an underlying biochemical problem that needs serious treatment."

As Merv told me a few days later, "I was stunned sitting there and looking at my grown-up daughter, whom I thought I had to protect all this time. She'd been dealing with her husband's problems quite intelligently. She was way ahead of me on this one."

I applauded Merv for realizing that he was going to need to treat his daughter with respect and to find a way to be of service to her without undermining her strength. Then I asked him an even tougher question: "Would you be willing to attend a counseling session in which Gerard is invited to tell his side of the story to you and your wife? My experience has been that addicts and troubled family members don't like to be lectured at, but they do show up and sometimes they even become somewhat more cooperative if the family promises to listen finally to what their own struggle is like."

Merv glared at me with the same "just bit into tinfoil" look again. Then he took a deep breath and said, "If that's what it takes."

"I Don't Want to Keep Messing Up"

A week later Gerard walked into my office with the understanding that the other family members were required to listen while he explained his own point of view about his longtime struggle with mood swings and drinking. As I've found with many addicted individuals, Gerard was a lot more pleasant to be around when he sensed that he was going to be listened to rather than when he thought he was going to be outnumbered or criticized.

At this family session I asked Gerard a version of the nonthreatening and usually successful question that was discussed earlier in Chapters Two and Three: "Would you be willing to tell your in-laws what you believe works and what doesn't work for making things healthier and less contentious in your family?"

For a few minutes, Gerard began to complain about all the times Merv and Gladys had been condescending or controlling toward him and Julianne. He was expecting Merv to disagree or cut him off, but instead Merv just listened. After a few minutes, Gerard relaxed a bit and then he turned to Julianne and said, "I don't want to keep messing up and making things hard for you and the kids. I know I've got a problem, but I absolutely will not go into some program where they require me to believe in something spiritual or religious. That's just not who I am."

At that moment I sensed that Gerard was as open to change as he was ever going to be. Even though I happen to be a person who loves the twelve-step programs that help men and women focus on their higher power (in whatever way they imagine that higher power to exist), I recognize that for a sizeable percentage of individuals the spiritual terminology is off-putting. So I suggested to Gerard, "Would you be willing to check out any recovery programs that don't insist on phrases you don't feel comfortable using? There are a few in our area that have helped a lot of people like yourself. One uses acupuncture and holistic remedies to help people stop drinking. Another uses nonreligious approaches to help people manage their cravings and addictions."

Gerard looked at me with a bit of hesitation and an equal measure of interest. He took a deep breath and said, "I'll check out one or two and see what they're like."

I complimented Gerard on his courage. "It takes guts to tackle these issues. I'm sure there are going to be some difficult moments as part of your recovery. But this is one of the most important things you've ever done for yourself, your wife, and your kids."

Gerard smiled. It was the first time I'd seen his face light up in a smile.

We could have stopped there, but I didn't want to focus just on the drinking. Quite often our troubled family members need help with more than one thing if they are gong to be successful in their recovery. So I asked Gerard and Julianne if they'd be willing during the next few months to start an anger management course designed for parents of young children, and also to consult with a psychiatrist who is an expert at medication for bipolar disorders. Gerard reacted immediately with reluctance and said, "Do I look rich? How am I gonna afford to pay for all this?"

At that point, Merv spoke up. He said, "Gerard, as you probably know I have a tendency to get in there and try to control everything. So you're gonna have to let me know if I'm getting too involved in your personal stuff. But I would be happy to pay for any anger management course or psychiatric bills that your insurance won't cover. This is not just for you and Julianne. This is for the grandkids, too."

Gerard thought for a moment and then said, "Merv, let me talk to Julianne and we'll let you know if we need any help."

Merv looked at me and then looked back at Gerard, saying, "There's a part of me that wants to say, 'You guys need to do what I think is right,' and there's a part of me that's beginning to realize I'm not in control here. I'm totally dependent on you and Julianne making things work. I don't like it when I'm not the one in charge, but I guess that's what I'm going to have to learn to live with. All I can say is I'm here if you need any help and I'm hoping you won't be too proud to ask."

Gerard smiled at his father-in-law and said, "I appreciate that, Merv. I know this hasn't been easy for any of us."

I can't promise that even half of the problem drinkers and drug users in our families will be as willing as Gerard was to try a healthier alternative. Experience tells me that close to half of all people with addictions simply are unwilling or unable to follow through on positive changes. But what worked for Merv, Gladys, Julianne, and Gerard is the same basic principle that has worked for many others. We need to stop trying to control or demonize the addicted person and explore creative options for those who haven't been successful yet in their recoveries. We live in a time when there are numerous twelve-step programs and alternative therapies that are quite effective. Without getting into a power struggle, simply give your troubled family member the information and encouragement he needs to make his own choice.

The other important lesson from this case is that a substantial percentage of people who are drawn to alcohol, drugs, gambling, and other habits are essentially trying to self-medicate and get relief from their underlying depression, anxiety, mood swings, shyness, physical discomforts, or emotional insecurities. Rather than judging or condemning this wounded individual, it might be more effective to understand that he or she didn't set out to become an addict. In most cases the drinking, drugs, or gambling is just a form of relief or escape that went too far and took on a biochemical urgency that is hard to resist. Seeing this person's addiction as a hard-to-change biochemical problem takes some of the shame and stigma out of the addiction. It can allow your family member to save face while seeking treatment for a "chemical imbalance" rather than for a failing of character.

Don't Overreact to Each Incident

A third and final issue of concern for the caring family members of people with addictions is how to deal with each setback, detour, relapse, or slip. Each time your troubled relative makes some progress you will be tempted to think or feel, "The worst is over. We're on our way to success." And each time your troubled relative has a setback, you will be tempted to think or feel, "Here we go again. There's no hope."

Rather than bouncing between these two extremes, it helps to see the recovery process in more accurate terms as a complicated mixture of daily steps forward and occasional steps backward. Even the strongest and most highly motivated individuals will still have cravings, urges, and possibly relapses or slips. Your job is not to be shocked, horrified, or pessimistic when these setbacks do occur.

"Every Few Months There's Another Desperate Phone Call"

Gillian is a thirty-one-year-old mother of two young children who has spent much of her life trying to help her troubled mom, Kristina, a very attractive and charming woman in her fifties who lights up a room wherever she goes. As Gillian described her, "My mother has always been able to land great jobs and attract some exciting boyfriends. But her recurring bouts with alcohol, drugs, and gambling have caused her to get fired from several of these jobs, and each relationship turns into ugly fights, angry separations, desperate attempts at reconciliation, and eventual messy breakups. I feel sorry for my mom because she's so dynamic and yet so fragile."

Gillian came for counseling a few years ago because, in her own words, "The constant drama from my mama is wearing me down. I try to get some distance from her but she's still my mother and when she calls with some sort of crisis or heartbreaking story I feel right back in the same old trap, trying to parent a stubborn woman who has never grown up. I try to focus on my own work, my own two kids, and my husband. But every few months there's another desperate phone call where my mom needs emergency cash, a plane ticket home, or even a ride to a doctor's office because she's gotten bruised up by one of her boyfriends. Every time the phone rings, I feel this huge adrenalin rush and I worry that we're in a crisis once again."

Gillian continued, "My mom has been in several treatment programs and she always wins the award for Miss Congeniality, snookering the staff into believing she's sincere and motivated. But a few weeks later we invariably get a phone call from Vegas or Atlantic City, or even Monte Carlo, and it's my dear old mom, in trouble again. If I let her, my mom is going to put us into serious financial trouble from all the times we get stuck paying her gambling and other debts. Plus all the times we turn our lives upside down to come and rescue her from some messy disaster. It's starting to affect my job, my marriage, and my sanity to always be responding to my mom's crises."

Like many of us who have addicted family members that slip and relapse every so often, Gillian needed help in three areas: what to do when her mom calls with another "emergency"; when to say "Yes, I'll help up to a limit"; and how to say with less guilt, "No, Mom, you've got to do that for yourself or with someone else's help besides mine."

These are tough choices, and I don't think there are simple answers that apply to all situations. But I'll describe what Gillian and I developed as her "keep the sanity" approach to her difficult mom. Then you can decide for yourself (or with the help of your own advisors) what strategies to use when your family member relapses or has a dramatic crisis that tugs at you.

The goal is to combine sincere compassion with realistic limit setting. Some people lean too far on the side of unlimited compassion and their addicted relatives often treat them like pushovers. On the other hand, some people lean too far on the side of cold limit setting or angry toughness and they miss out on chances to be of assistance to a troubled family member who could truly benefit from a warmer approach. In between the two extremes is a large middle zone of compassionate limit setting. It's not always easy to figure out what your limits are or how to set them in a compassionate way. But if you master this essential skill, you will not only learn how to deal more effectively with an addicted relative but with every other manipulative individual in your life, including volatile teenage children, dishonest ex-spouses, pushy neighbors, and saccharine snakes at work. The practice you will gain setting compassionate limits with your troubled family member can prepare you for many other challenges in life where you will need to be simultaneously strong but loving.

Here are the three steps that Gillian tried out for staying sane in spite of what she liked to call her "drama mama:"

Step 1: Decide ahead of time what you're willing to do and what is too much. Gillian and her husband, Lawrence, sat down and decided ahead of time what they would do the next time Gillian's mother called with a financial crisis or other emergency. They weighed several possibilities of what they believed a good son-in-law and daughter should do for a relapsing family member with a gambling and substance abuse problem. They eventually decided that based on their own financial situation and their other family responsibilities, they would set aside a limited budget of six hundred dollars per year for helping Kristina if she got in a crisis, and be willing to take a maximum of one long car ride or plane trip each year to help Kristina if she got into a jam and needed immediate assistance.

As Gillian explained it, "My husband and I didn't want

to be cruel or cold, but we also didn't want my mother's chaotic life to continue to keep us in debt or force us to be unable to do all we wanted to do for our own children. So we decided on a reasonable amount of yearly help we could offer and we wrote my mother a respectful and considerate letter telling her that while we love her enormously, we also don't have unlimited money or time to assist her when she's in crisis. We told her how sorry we were to have to admit we are human, but we do need to set a yearly maximum during the foreseeable future."

A few days after she sent the letter, Gillian called me to say, "My mom got the letter and she's pissed. But you warned us she would be pissed. And I do think we were quite decent and loving in the way we told her up front what we could do to help and what would be too much to expect of us."

As often happens when we set compassionate limits with an addicted relative, Kristina gave Gillian the silent treatment for several days. I assured Gillian, however, "There's a ninety-eight percent chance that she'll call as soon as she misses you or needs you." Sure enough, ten days later Gillian and Lawrence got a desperate phone call from Kristina asking for help with Kristina's laptop computer, which Lawrence is good at fixing. As Gillian told me, "My mom never even mentioned our earlier disagreement about the limits we were setting. She just acted as if nothing had happened. We were right back to business as usual with my mom, except that now we had warned her that we are human and we do have limits."

Step 2: Become a loving brick wall during tough times. Whether intentionally or simply by virtue of being a distressed addict, your family member will almost certainly test your limits—over and over again. What I urge counseling clients to do is to practice ahead of time saying silently to yourself a few magic words that can help you stay focused and strong during a difficult moment with your addicted family member. These magic words are, "Loving brick wall. Loving brick wall." By saying these few words silently to yourself at least two times, you prepare your mind to be firm but compassionate with anyone who is trying to push you past your limits. Then when your distressed family member actually tries to use a guilt trip to get you to ignore the limits you've had to set, you will have a powerful antidote that can keep you centered and compassionate.

At the precise moment when you are on the phone or talking in person with this troubled family member who is trying to get you to do something unreasonable to help him or her during a crisis, you can say to yourself silently, "Loving brick wall. Loving brick wall." Instead of yelling angrily at your relative or else acting like a passive victim, just saying those words can help you stay focused as you restate your limits.

For example, the first "loving brick wall" test for Gillian came eight weeks after she sent her mother the letter spelling out the limits that would apply during a crisis. Her mother, Kristina, called from Laughlin, Nevada, to say that she had been arrested for writing bad checks on her employer's bank account to cover some huge gambling debts. Upset and talking rapidly, Kristina wanted Gillian and her husband to drive or fly immediately to Laughlin to bail her out for ten thousand dollars and also to help her pay for a lawyer to "beat these ridiculous charges."

Normally Gillian would have dropped everything to rush in and try to help her troubled mom. But this time Gillian took a deep breath and silently said to herself the centering words we had practiced, "Loving brick wall. Loving brick wall." Then she said audibly and calmly into the phone, "Mom, I love you and I'm sorry you're in a horrible spot right now. I wish we could do more to help. But as we talked about eight weeks ago, the most we can come up with is six hundred dollars per year for emergency expenses like a lawyer. We also need to make sure we don't jeopardize our jobs and our kids by rushing over there to Laughlin. I'm able to make an emergency trip once a year, but not more than that. Do you think this should be the time for me to cancel work, get a babysitter for the kids, and come be with you? I'll do it if it's absolutely necessary. Or do you want me to save up my one time off from work in case you need it later on?"

"You can shove it up your ass," was Kristina's reply. "I don't want you here if that's your attitude."

Gillian said silently, "Loving brick wall. Loving brick wall." Then she said audibly and warmly into the phone, "Listen to me, Mom. I love you and I care about you a lot. But you're gonna need to live with the consequences of writing bad checks on your boss's bank account. I didn't do that and Lawrence didn't do that. You did that, and I'm gonna be on your side no matter what. If you need more than six hundred dollars it's gonna have to come from some of your other friends and relatives this time. I'm so sorry. I wish I could do more, but you and I already talked about this. Lawrence and I are human and we have to set some healthy limits."

Kristina was crying as she said, "Why are you doing this to me? I'm your mother . . ."

Gillian took a deep breath and slowed down her racing blood pressure by repeating silently the words, "Loving brick wall. Loving brick wall." Then she said to her mother, "I'm doing this because I care about you. I've got two kids, a husband, a job, and financial realities. I wish I could do a lot more to help, but I truly believe that you'll find a way to learn and grow from this. I just hope we can stay close no matter what because I love you and you'll always be my mom."

Kristina swore and hung up the phone at that point. But she called the next day to say, "I'm sorry. I was a bit hungover last night. I know you love me and I didn't mean some of the things I said to you."

As I've found with many counseling clients who have had to set limits with their addicted relatives, it's never easy. But the challenge is to be realistic about what you can offer and what will push you over the edge into resentment or financial troubles. Even if your relative puts up a fuss, it's far more decent to be honest and compassionate, to be a "loving brick wall," than to let someone push you past your limits, which will usually destroy the relationship with feelings of bitterness and victimization. The best way to keep loving a troubled or addicted person is to remind her that you exist and that you are going to take good care of yourself so that you don't burn out or get destroyed by the chaos.

Step 3: Get support so you can be a consistent and strong ally (but never a doormat) for your troubled relative. With each relapse, emergency, or crisis you will be tested. If you do your best to breathe, stay calm, and accept that your compassionate limits are not mean, you will probably be able to weather the storms and keep your sanity. You may need the wisdom, experience, and fellowship of others in an Al-Anon or some other caregiver support program. You may need to pray a lot or call supportive friends each time you begin wondering, "Is it wrong to say no to someone who's making unreasonable demands? Is it cruel to tell an addicted family member that we're all human and we have limits, too?"

In Gillian's case, getting support from Al-Anon was especially important because Kristina kept trying to blame Gillian and her husband for her own legal difficulties. For several days after her arrest, Kristina kept calling and insisting she wanted them to come to Laughlin with ten thousand dollars to bail her out. Gillian stayed strong, however, and told her mother, "I'll help you find a great attorney and I'll pay the first six hundred dollars of legal fees. But the rest of the money is going to have to come from your other friends and relatives." Kristina wound up borrowing most of the legal costs from one of her ex-boyfriends, and she put up a good defense before being sentenced to six months in jail and a moderate-sized fine for forging the checks.

Despite how painful it was to know how unhappy her mom was in jail, Gillian found that, "After the first few months in prison my mom seemed to grow up a bit from the double whammy of my setting limits on her and also from being in a place where they didn't care how good looking or charming she was. I think the boring prison clothes, the bad food, and the fact that my husband and I continued to give her emotional support with weekly phone calls and visits got my mom to realize that we do love her. One afternoon I was sitting with her in the women's prison visiting area and I heard her say to me, 'Gillian, you're a tough one sometimes, but I'm glad you're strong. Because if you weren't strong, I would probably have worn you out by now.'"

Gillian said of her mom, "I think she became somewhat humbled from being in jail and that's helped her get serious about working toward recovery. So far during the first twelve months since she's gotten out of prison, she's stayed sober, stopped gambling, and worked hard at her new job. I can't predict the future, but I'm glad my husband and I got out of the business of doing too much for my mom and then re-senting her for it. This whole ordeal has taught me a lot about patience, firmness, and being able to set limits lovingly, which

I'm probably gonna need with my kids when they become teenagers. And I've finally found a way to just love my mom and not carry the full burden of trying to rescue her. Only Kristina can rescue Kristina, with the love and support of all of us who have stuck by her. Most importantly, I think I'm finally starting to learn that she's supposed to be the mom and I'm supposed to be the daughter. It took a long time to figure out that my job is not to take away all of her problems. My job is to let her know that I care about her and that I'm only human."

If you, too, have a family member who sometimes brings chaos to your life or who frequently tests your limits, my hope is that this stressful relationship will sooner or later bring you crucial insights like it did for Gillian and many others I have counseled. Our most troubled relatives often indirectly cause us to learn about patience, persistence, limit setting, and compassion. I wish there were an easier way to learn these important things, but for now all we can do is appreciate that our addicted relatives might be helping us grow much more than we ever thought possible.

CHAPTER EIGHT

IS THERE ANYTHING YOU CAN DO ABOUT RELATIVES WHO ARE INTOLERANT?

Have you ever witnessed any overt or subtle racism in your family? For example, is there someone in your family who tends to say condescending or contemptuous things about people of other races? Or possibly someone in your family who has what is called "internalized racism" and can't stop criticizing or seeing only the worst traits in your own race or ethnic group?

Have you detected any severe or mild sexism in your family? Is there someone in your family who says hostile things toward women who aren't passive and sweet all the time? Does he try to feel big by making cruel jokes or insensitive comments at family gatherings? Is there someone who gives first-class treatment and lots of encouragement to one gender, but gives second-class treatment and harsh criticism to members of the other gender?

Have you noticed any homophobic remarks or insulting comments about sexual orientation in your family? Do you have a relative who tries to enforce very strict limits as to what is proper for a boy and what is proper for a girl for fear that someone might be "different?" Or a family member who would be uncomfortable if you introduced her to someone who is gay, lesbian, bisexual, or transgendered? (A transgendered person is someone who feels more at home in the clothes, behavior, or actual body of the other gender.) Have you ever gotten into a frustrating argument with a family member about homosexuality and felt as if the conversation went nowhere?

If you answered yes to any of the above questions, you are not alone. Over the years I've found that nearly every family has at least one of these kinds of conflicts. Even if no single relative flaunts the fact that he's racist, sexist, or homophobic, I'm willing to bet there might still be some of these feelings just under the surface. Quite often people think they've moved beyond the prejudices and intolerance of past generations, but then a family member announces that he's in love with someone very different from what the family had been expecting. At those moments, powerful feelings may flare up unexpectedly, and sometimes we hear loved ones say things we never thought we'd hear.

This chapter will explore a controversial topic that I have rarely seen addressed in books on personal growth or family relations: not so much the politics of racism, sexism, and homophobia, but more the personal side of these issues. I'd also like to introduce you to approaches that can help you deal with hurtful comments that you witness—or are the target of—in your own family.

HOW TO RESPOND TO A PREJUDICED RELATIVE

If someone in your family says or does something that offends you (or is intolerant or hurtful toward someone you care about), should you simply ignore it? Should you just shrug it off and say, "My relative is insensitive and closed-minded. There's nothing I can do about it." Or would you like to be able to respond in an effective way?

For more than twenty years I have been a consultant and advisor for several human relations organizations on the family aspects and psychological roots of intolerance. My focus has been on how to respond when someone in your family causes you pain because he or she is hostile or mistrustful toward a certain group of people. I have found over the years that if you want to make an impact on your intolerant relative, there are three specific approaches that dramatically improve your chances.

Clarify Your Own Reasons for Caring about the Issue

Quite often people who feel hurt by an offensive remark become self-righteous and immediately start name-calling or judging the relative who made the remark. "You're such a racist," or "You sexist pig," or "You are seriously homophobic" might be your or another family member's response. Within seconds, the conversation turns into an ugly argument or the person has tuned you out. Instead of making an impact on your hurtful relative, that person puts up an emotional wall and thinks to himself, "I'm right and this ridiculous bleeding-heart, politically correct jerk in front of me is wrong."

That's why I recommend trying something less political and more personal. The most powerful thing you can do in response to a hurtful remark is to stop, take a breath, and then clarify in a heart-to-heart way why you are so hurt or upset by what was just said or done. It requires being honest and vulnerable, which might not be your first reaction to an intolerant or bigoted relative. But if you take a moment to check into your own feelings regarding this issue, you will find it often leads to much greater practical success.

"I've Never Gotten Honest with You about This"

For example, one of my counseling clients is Robert, a twenty-eight-year-old African-American schoolteacher who grew up in an upwardly mobile family where his hardworking parents thought they were being fair to each of their three children. But in fact, according to Robert, as the darkest-skinned member of the family he tended to receive less affection, less attention, and less encouragement than his two lighter-skinned siblings. "I know my parents and grandparents loved me," said Robert, "but they had much higher hopes and confidence in my brother and sister who could 'pass' more easily in affluent circles. When I was very little my mother used to look at me and say, in a sad voice, 'He's too dark, just like my no-good grandpa used to be.'"

Robert continued, "During high school, my brother and sister were told they should go to fancy colleges back East and I was told that, despite my good grades, the local state college was good enough for me. My father admitted once, 'There ain't no way a Fortune 500 company is gonna recruit someone who looks like you.' And when my dad's father passed away, he left a somewhat larger sum to both of my siblings, as if to say to me, 'You're a risky investment; we all think your brother and sister can go much further in life.'"

Recently Robert's father was being honored by the local Rotary Club for his ten years of membership in the organization, and for being the only African American in their suburban chapter. Robert's mom said to Robert when he was getting dressed before the event, "Do me a favor tonight at the dinner, Robert. Don't give anybody that angry black look of yours. Try to be nice."

Immediately, Robert said what he has said many times before. "Mom, you are such a racist." Just as quickly, his mother tuned him out and said dismissively, "Yeah, right."

Robert persisted. "You really are a racist. I'm not kidding." His mom cut him off and said, "Just get dressed,

Robert. And save your high and mighty political speeches for your students at school."

When Robert came in for counseling the next week, he was furious at his mom. This incident had triggered a host of memories of times when Robert felt he had been treated as a second-class citizen by his own family. We had a long talk about how the internalized racism in Robert's family had caused his upwardly mobile relatives to underestimate Robert's potential, and to come down extra hard on him because of his darker skin and stronger features.

Then we discussed what might help his mother and father to understand just how painful it was to be on the receiving end of their dismissive racial comments. I asked Robert if he'd be willing to stop calling his parents "racists" and start trying something more effective instead.

Robert argued, "But they *are* racists. Why can't I just say the truth to them?"

I explained to Robert, "It's easier to call our relatives a political label like 'racist' or 'sexist,' but it only causes them to roll their eyes and ignore your legitimate concerns. What's harder but often more effective is to dig deep inside and be willing to let your family members see the unintended harm their words can cause. In order for this to work successfully, you will need to remind your mom and dad that you know they do care about you and that you assume they don't want to hurt you. You may need to admit to them that you're vulnerable and human. For many people, that's a much harder thing to say than to just blurt out the word 'racist.'"

Robert remarked, "It's definitely a harder thing to say. I mean, why should I have to be the one to get vulnerable when my mother is saying hurtful things? She's the one who's wrong, and yet you want me to remind her that I know she loves me and doesn't want to hurt me."

"That's exactly right," I said. "It's hard to stay loving and centered right when you're facing the person who has just hurt you. But if you can do that and if you can remind your mother just how much she does care about you, then you've got a chance to penetrate her heart and get her to see why her comments about skin color are so destructive and inappropriate."

A few days later, Robert tried out what we had discussed. He took his mother to lunch on the weekend and said, "I know you care about me and that you don't really want to hurt me. But when you or Dad talk about my skin and make it sound like I'm a lesser person than my brother and sister because of something I can't control, it hurts a lot. It makes me want to put up a wall and close myself off from the family, which is not what I really wanna do. I've never gotten honest with you about this—about how hard it is for me when you start associating me with your messed-up grandpa and his dark skin. I'm *not* him, and times are different from what he was facing when he grew up in Mississippi sixty years ago. Please, Mom, you've got to think twice before you let my skin cause you to underestimate who I am. It's not good for me as a person and it's not good for us as a family if you keep making decisions based on who's dark and who's light."

To Robert's surprise, his words traveled deeply into his mother's heart. He told me a few days after his conversation with his mother, "I saw her face get real tense and I wasn't sure if she was going to be angry or defensive or what. But then I saw a couple of tears start trickling down from her eyes. My mother rarely gets vulnerable, but for a minute she looked at me with such caring. It was like she was seeing me, the real me, for the first time."

If you decide to utilize this first approach of being vulnerable and clarifying exactly why the racist, sexist, or homophobic remarks are hurtful to you personally, please know that your family member might still put up a wall. He or she might be unable or unwilling to face the fact that certain remarks can hurt someone unintentionally.

However, if you remind this person again that you know she does care about you and that you assume she doesn't really want to cause you pain, you will have a much better chance of breaking through the defensiveness and getting heard. I've found that even the most bigoted, intolerant, and insensitive human beings have a heart, but in some cases it's covered over with layers of emotional scar tissue and hardness. You will be taking a risk when you open up and admit your vulnerable feelings to this person, but it's the most powerful way to crack the layers of protection and defensiveness surrounding this person's fragile ego.

Find the Good Side of This Person

A second approach that I have found works to break an impasse with intolerant or rigid relatives is what I call "meeting them exactly where they are." Here's how it works.

Instead of reacting against a particular viewpoint that you find offensive, why not accept that your family member is probably going to continue to hold this viewpoint, at least to some extent. Instead of trying to remake this person into a clone of you and your values, try to communicate with him in a way that's not threatening, and that shows respect for his deeper values and beliefs.

For instance, what if you or someone in your extended family is gay or lesbian and one or more of your relatives thinks that same-sex intimacy is forbidden by the Bible. Instead of trying to convince this family member to stop being religious or to ignore the teachings of his minister or spiritual teacher, what if you were willing to honor this person's religious values and at the same time to help him see a way to be more compassionate and accepting of the family member who is gay? This may sound hard to do, but I have seen huge breakthroughs in even some of the most dogmatic families using this approach.

"I Don't Want Our Family to Be Ripped Apart Like This"

Elana's case is a good illustration of how to make this happen. Elana is a forty-year-old writer and mom whose seventeen-year-old son, Ari, recently announced to the family that he is gay. Elana is a Reform Jew who is mostly comfortable with her son's sexual orientation, even though she worries about how he'll be treated in the larger world. She came in for counseling, however, because she has felt frustrated and upset at some of the remarks and reactions she's gotten from her older brother Sid, a tradition-oriented person who grew up Orthodox and is now the president of his Conservative synagogue. On the day Elana called me to make a counseling appointment, she had gotten into a shouting match on the phone with Sid, who told her, "This is a *shanda* (a shameful scandal). You've got to do something to help Ari. It's not too late, and frankly you've been letting him act like a fag for way too long."

Elana told me during her first session, "It breaks my heart to see how this could split our family into factions. If push comes to shove, I will definitely side with my son, even if it means we stop having family get-togethers and holidays with Sid and his four obsessively high-achieving children. But I don't want our family to be ripped apart like this. Our parents were Holocaust survivors and we lost most of our relatives in the concentration camps. The truth is I love Sid, even though he can be a real pain in the ass sometimes."

When I asked Elana what she hoped counseling might accomplish, she said, "I wish I could get Sid to stop being such a holy roller with all of his rigid beliefs. I wish I could say to my arrogant older brother, 'C'mon already. This is America and it's the twenty-first century. Stop thinking and acting like you're living in some narrow-minded Jewish ghetto in Europe a hundred years ago.'"

Rather than encourage Elana to try to change Sid from a tradition-oriented Jew into a Reform Jew (which Elana told me was as likely to happen as the Pope appointing a Jewish cardinal), I asked her if she would be willing to honor Sid's beliefs even while helping him to be more compassionate. Elana said reluctantly, "If I have to honor his beliefs, it won't kill me."

So we began to discuss three ways to help a religiously observant Jew deal with these complex issues. First, I suggested to Elana that she assist her brother in understanding the dictionary definition of the word "faggot," which refers to a bundle of wooden sticks to be burned as fuel. Some experts say this term originated in Europe in the Middle Ages when certain Christian clergy and civic leaders began tying up homosexuals and burning them in the town square. I said to Elana, "After you explain the original meaning and history to Sid, see if he would ever use that hurtful word again, especially in light of your family's experiences in the Holocaust." Quite often if you help a family member see the horrific history that underlies an insulting word he has been using casually, it will cause him to stop using it. I've found this to be true for the majority of people who get told respectfully the origins of the word "faggot."

Second, I gave Elana a series of religious position papers, articles, and speeches put together by Rabbi Elliott Dorff, who is the rector of the University of Judaism and a highly respected Conservative scholar of Jewish religious law. Like most Reform rabbis and some Conservative rabbis, Elliott Dorff has spoken out in favor of gay and lesbian rights and the need for gay and lesbian clergy. After studying the religious issues involved in interpreting Leviticus 20 and the other Biblical and post-Biblical statements about homosexuality, Dorff and many of his colleagues have concluded that certain compassionate commandments and rulings take precedence over the earlier interpretations that reflected ancient discomforts about same-sex relations. Dorff has said, "Whatever Leviticus was prohibiting was assuming that a person has the ability to do otherwise, because if you don't have the ability to do otherwise it doesn't make logical or legal sense to prohibit it." Dorff and many others have argued that in light of recent scientific studies that show the majority of gays, lesbians, and bisexuals are trying to live up to their God-given way of expressing love and commitment, it would be wrong to judge or criticize them for it.

In addition, Rabbi Bradley Artson, the dean of the Conservative movement's rabbinical school at the University of Judaism, argues that Leviticus 20:13, which says that a man should not lie down with another man, was referring to promiscuous, oppressive, or cultic homosexual practices that were common at the time of the Bible and was never meant to refer to loving, monogamous homosexual relationships.

Elana examined these and other commentaries from traditional Jewish scholars and then said to me, "I had no idea how seriously religious Jews were wrestling with such issues. I'd always thought that people who were traditional were just closed-minded, but this makes me wonder if maybe I was wrong. There seem to be quite a few Jewish scholars and rabbis who are struggling to reconcile the ancient teachings with modern wisdom. Studying these texts and these interpretations makes me respect my brother Sid a little more because Sid has always been willing to go back and study with a variety of teachers and scholars to make sense of the Torah (the Hebrew Bible) as it applies to modern life."

Third, Elana and I explored together how much both traditional Jews like Sid and liberal Jews like Elana emphasize family closeness and the holiness of lifelong commitments. I asked her, "Do you think Sid would be interested in stretching a little to keep your family together celebrating the holidays and life cycle events each year? Do you think he would be willing to dance and sing with you if Ari finds a life partner in the next few years and invites Sid and his family to a commitment ceremony or even a marriage conducted by a Reform or Conservative rabbi?"

Elana's eyes filled up with tears as she imagined the possibility of her brother celebrating her son's joyous occasion. She said, "I haven't always been into prayer, but I will definitely pray for and visualize the day when Ari is exchanging vows and Sid is giving him a hug and saying, 'Mazel tov!'"

It took several weeks and a few stressful conversations

before Sid shifted his stance and agreed to accept his nephew Ari. On the day when Sid finally invited Elana, Ari, and the other relatives over for Sabbath dinner, Sid toasted his sister and his nephew and then said with a mischievous grin on his face, "The past few weeks have been a bit of a miracle. First of all, yours truly became even more of a *mensch* (a good person). Second, I got to see my very liberal sister Elana sit down and study from traditional Jewish texts, and she was even taking Jewish law somewhat seriously for once in her life. That's definitely a miracle. And finally, I got to know my nephew Ari much better than I ever have. He's a good person, and I'm grateful that his honesty and his courage have made this family stronger and closer than we've ever been."

"We Want Our Families to Continue to Love Us"

A similar family dilemma that I encountered seven months ago involved a young woman named Ginger, who came to a church speech I gave on dealing with family conflicts. Ginger is a twenty-four-year-old graduate student in social work who grew up in a fundamentalist Baptist family and discovered at the age of twenty-two that she was madly in love with a class-mate named Amelia, who grew up in a strict Catholic family.

Unsure of whether or not to trust her strong feelings for Amelia, Ginger tried to pretend it was just a phase or a temporary "passing fancy." She even consulted with her family's minister, who warned her that if she acted on her desires she would be jeopardizing her salvation.

On the other hand, Amelia felt ready after a few months to move in together and make a commitment to Ginger. She had been comfortable with her own sexual orientation ever since her first crushes on women in high school and college. Amelia worried, however, that Ginger might be a LUG—a Lesbian Until Graduation who is strongly attracted to women but who goes back to a more conventional relationship eventually. Ginger and Amelia were both concerned about the rejection and bad feelings they might face from their families.

Then, after two years of trying hard to suppress her feelings and replace her romantic attraction for Amelia with Bible readings and church attendance, Ginger came across a passage in the Bible that made her begin to cry uncontrollably. The passage said simply, "And the truth shall set you free."

Ginger told me during a private conversation on the day of my speech at the Unity church she had joined, "That Biblical passage got to me in such a deep place. I realized at that moment when reading the Bible that my truth has always been a spiritual desire to be in a committed loving relationship with a woman. My first crushes in elementary school and middle school were toward girls I admired. I tried desperately to become attracted to boys and I even had a steady boyfriend for a year in high school. But my deepest longing was to love a woman, and I decided the day I read those words in the Bible that it was time to stop pretending otherwise."

As she had feared, this revelation caused an enormous amount of tension in Ginger's family. A few weeks later her dad found out she had been seen holding hands with Amelia in a restaurant. He immediately cut off her tuition payments and living expenses. Ginger's mom called her a slut and said she was going to hell. Her older brother Ray tried to get her to see a "conversion therapist" who attempts to reprogram people to change their romantic feelings from one gender to the other.

In Amelia's family there was less drama, but she noticed "a feeling of coldness and distance had set in. My parents and my two sisters tried to act as if they were fine with my coming out, but you could tell they were very uncomfortable. At one point my younger sister said, 'Why did you have to go and do this to Mom and Dad? Can't you see how disappointed this has made them?'"

During Ginger and Amelia's first counseling session in my office, I had asked them, "What is the best outcome you would want from this counseling?" Ginger and Amelia both agreed, "We want our families to continue to love us."

After spending several sessions exploring the tensions that each had experienced in her respective family, I asked Ginger and Amelia, "What if I told you that we were going to have to take your family members' beliefs and discomforts seriously? What if I told you they might not ever feel fully comfortable or accepting of who you are?"

Ginger and Amelia looked at each other, and then Ginger said, "We've talked a lot about how much we don't want to hurt our families. Yet we're also committed to being together and making a lifelong promise to build a healthy family, maybe even with one or two children. I guess we're going to have to deal with our relatives exactly where they are and accept that this is going to be hard for many, if not all, of them."

Amelia added, "I love my family and I've wanted them to accept and appreciate that I've found an amazing partner for life. But I have to accept that they may or may not be able to go against their fears that say Ginger and I are doing something wrong."

Having reached an acceptance that their relatives might not change, Ginger and Amelia were now ready to talk to them in a heart-to-heart way. During the next few weeks, both women began discussing with each of their key relatives how much they wanted their family's love and how they knew this was not an easy issue for any of them. I urged Ginger and Amelia to open up the one-on-one conversations with each of their relatives by saying in their own words what kind of closeness and mutual respect they hoped for, even if their relatives were not able to accept them completely.

Here's what Ginger said: "I care about you and I want you to know that I will always treasure the family closeness we've had together. So please let me know whatever concerns or questions arise because of what I've told you about who I really am. Or if you want to talk to someone with more experience in these matters than I have, there's a chapter of Parents and Friends of Lesbians and Gays (PFLAG) that meets once a month in a church not far from dad's office. I want to respect your feelings and your struggles with this. Even if at times we're going to see things differently, I hope we can do our best to treat each other like family and to learn and grow from all of this."

I also helped Ginger and Amelia find some copies of articles, speeches, and other writings that spelled out how various Protestant and Catholic clergy and scholars are addressing the complicated issue of how to be a compassionate Christian when dealing with family members and friends who are gay. Specifically, I asked Ginger and Amelia to offer any of their relatives who were interested a choice of three different written viewpoints on the issue: one from a minister who is convinced that homosexuality is an unforgivable sin; one from a minister who is convinced that same-sex committed relationships are holy and sacred; and one from a minister who argues strongly for church-sponsored gay and lesbian commitment ceremonies and civil rights but is reluctant to support same-sex marriages.

I told Ginger and Amelia, "Let your relatives look over these various points of view on the issue and know that each of these Christian theologians takes the Bible and church tradition very seriously. Then let your relatives consult with their own clergy and pray in their own hearts for guidance on how to respond to your request for closeness and respect."

It took a lot of courage and persistence for Amelia and Ginger to participate in these difficult discussions, particularly with some of their relatives. But over the next few weeks

Ginger discovered that "My family is a lot more diverse than I realized. My older brother Ray continued to insist he was horrified by my 'sinful lifestyle choice' and would hope that I reconsider. My aunt wanted to send me to a reprogramming camp where they try to convert people to heterosexuality. But my mom and dad shifted a little and were quite wonderful, saying, 'We really appreciate how loving and respectful you've been in letting us have our feelings and concerns about this. It's not going to be easy for us, and we're concerned about your soul. But we'll always love you.'"

Amelia described the situation in her family. "There's still a lot of politeness and condescension. Most of my relatives say they're being compassionate, but in actuality they just aren't willing to talk about how uncomfortable they are with all this. And then there's my outspoken grandmother, who said it best: 'I'm gonna let the priests and the scholars argue this one out. All I care about, Amelia, is that I thought you were a blessed gift from God the minute I saw you as a baby and I still think you're a blessed gift from God today. I can't wait to meet the lucky lady who gets to spend her life with someone as spectacular as you!'"

If sexual orientation is a controversial topic in your own family, I recommend the readings and resources listed in Sources and Suggested Readings on page 293. By encouraging your relatives to attend a PFLAG meeting where they can talk to other men and women who struggled with their own discomforts, a lot of healing can occur. Or, if you show respect for your relatives' viewpoints by sharing with them books or articles on the issue so that they can decide for themselves how they want to deal with their mixed feelings, quite often this will encourage them to be a little more respectful of who you are as well. I can't promise success in every case, but I have seen that there can be warmth and mutual respect among relatives, even when there are strongly conflicting viewpoints over serious issues.

Investigate the Psychology of the Person's Stance

When a family member rigidly refuses to loosen up about race, sexuality, or gender issues, there's usually something more going on. Without condoning or making excuses for this person's insulting comments, I would urge you to do some detective work to find out why this person is so unforgiving on this particular topic.

For example, if you examine the family history and early childhood experiences of men and women who tell racial jokes or feel hostile toward people of different races, you will often find one of three possibilities.

First possibility: This person may have been taught some extremely negative and exaggerated stereotypes as a child. Now, as an adult, it's as though by telling these racial jokes they are being loyal to the people or environment in which they grew up.

Second possibility: This person may have grown up in an insecure low-income household, or a formerly well-to-do family that was concerned about dropping in status, and so was told as a child, "We're struggling to get by, but we're better than [a certain minority group]." Then, as members of that minority group began passing him by on the highway of success or happiness, resentment started to grow.

Third possibility: This person may have had a painful experience with someone from that race or ethnicity, or was told stories about someone else's painful experiences, and this one incident was then generalized into a lifelong fear or contempt for members of that group.

If you do some research by talking with your parents, grandparents, aunts, siblings, or cousins about the member of your family who chronically tells racial jokes or makes racial slurs, you will probably find some useful information about how this person became so negative and hurtful. Once again, this research is not meant to excuse or justify his cruelty or insensitivity. Rather, it reveals the hidden wounds and beliefs that you will need to take seriously as you seek to discuss racial issues with this person.

"Do You Really Want Everyone to Think You're That Insecure?"

Let me give you an example from my own family about how it helps to understand the history and psychology of people if you want to make an impact on them regarding their obnoxious jokes or hostile comments.

I grew up in the 1960s in Detroit, where most of my

family members were liberal about civil rights and tended to be open-minded about people from different races and ethnicities. Yet I also have a cousin who grew up feeling intimidated and angry about the sudden influx of different races during her junior and senior years of high school. This cousin later married a man from a struggling low-income white family who it seems grew up so insecure that he desperately needs to feel superior to *someone*. So they've often interrupted family holiday conversations to tell unpleasant jokes about various races and ethnic groups. They think they're being funny, even though almost everyone else thinks they're being foolish. It appears that telling these "look how dumb those folks are" jokes about people of various races essentially keeps my cousin and her husband from feeling at the bottom of the social pecking order.

Each time this happens, several of us in the family try to get them to stop. I'd say we've made a sixty percent improvement in getting these two relatives to cut the racial remarks and jokes. But every so often they seem to revert to their old ways and once again they need to be confronted.

One time I was able get them to stop their racial remarks for almost a year. I had sat down next to them at a family gathering and said quietly, "You've worked hard to make a good living and raise a family. You don't need to put some other group down in order to know you're okay. All of us respect what you've done with your lives, but when you tell racial jokes or make racial remarks you each seem like a low-life again. I don't see why you'd want to do that. Do you really want everyone to think you're that insecure?"

That conversation was the first time I felt this cousin and her husband taking seriously how unpleasant the remarks and jokes are. It didn't make a permanent impact, because a year later my cousin and her husband once again were making racial jokes at the holiday dinner table. So once again I took them aside and asked them to look at how their jokes were intended to make them feel big but were actually making them look small. They were somewhat irritated at being confronted, yet it did wake them up again to the ugliness of what they're doing and caused them to cut out the jokes for a while.

"He Just Can't Stop Himself"

Camilla's case is one final example of what can happen if you take some time to consider the deeper reasons why one of your relatives is bigoted or intolerant. A highly creative and intelligent woman in her early thirties, Camilla grew up in a family where the women wash all the dishes after a holiday meal while the men drink heavily and watch sports on television without lifting a finger to help. The sons are encouraged to pursue lucrative careers, while the daughters are warned that too much independence and outspokenness will frighten away potential husbands.

Camilla has always wanted to get closer to her father, a very complicated man who can be extremely kind and generous with strangers but very cold and authoritarian with his five children. He's especially harsh with Camilla, his eldest child, and he's been very critical of her attempts to establish her own life. He also tends to make insulting remarks about Camilla's imperfect figure, her imperfect cooking, and her imperfect driving. When Camilla considered going away to college, her father insisted that she must stay close to home to take care of her younger siblings. When Camilla tried to start her own business as a graphic designer, her father refused to help her and he told her she didn't know the first thing about money and would never succeed. When Camilla voices an opinion or disagrees with her father, he'll say, "See, that's the reason why you'll never get a husband."

During our first counseling session, I asked Camilla how she responds to her father's comments. Camilla laughed and said, "I eat chocolate. Or sometimes I go into the freezer and knock off a carton of chocolate chip mint ice cream. My father is a sexist bastard, but for some reason I'm still trying to win his approval. Am I sick or what?"

After two counseling sessions in which we explored Camilla's business ideas and commitment to working hard to succeed in life, I asked her the following question: "Do you feel as if you will need your father's encouragement or do you think you will be able to succeed without it?"

Camilla became silent for a moment and then she said softly, "I desperately want his encouragement and I'm terrified I'll never get it."

That began a series of attempts to see if we could help her father recognize and acknowledge the hardworking and creative daughter he has. We tried approach number one, in which Camilla sat her father down and had a heart-to-heart talk about why his negative comments about women knowing nothing about business were holding her back. Her father listened impatiently and then said, "You're just like your mother. Way too sensitive. That's gonna hurt you in the business world. Mark my words."

We tried approach number two in which Camilla tried to meet her father exactly where he's at regarding women and equality. She told him she appreciated that his overprotectiveness came from a loving concern to shield his daughters from the stressful ups and downs of life. She told him she would always be his little girl, even if she was successful in her graphics business. She also told him she loved him and hoped he would continue to be a crucial advisor she could always ask for help and support.

But after each of these attempts to get closer, Camilla continued to receive a cold look of disapproval from her father. Rather than her father reciprocating with warmth and encouragement, Camilla described his response this way: "My father gets this distant look on his face as though he's feeling uncomfortable or is lost in his own thoughts. There I am, waiting like a stupid puppy dog for him to give me a bone, and he's sitting there all frozen emotionally. I hate him for it.

At those moments I wonder if he's capable of loving me at all or if he's just stuck having a pushy daughter who isn't the kind of person he had hoped for."

So Camilla and I decided it was time to do some research about why her father was this emotionally frozen and why he appeared to be unwilling to let down his guard with his eldest daughter. From talking with her paternal aunt and uncle, a few gems emerged. Camilla discovered from looking at one of her aunt's old photos of Camilla's father that when he was five years old there was a lightness and aliveness in his face that Camilla had never seen during her many years of knowing her father. But starting at the age of six, something changed for her father.

According to Camilla's aunt and uncle, what happened when her father was six is that his own father died suddenly and his family suffered a severe financial setback. They had to move from a spacious rural ranch to a tiny house in a crowded and crime-filled urban neighborhood. Camilla's grandmother became a domestic, working long hours cleaning up affluent people's homes and taking care of their affluent kids. Camilla's father and his siblings were left at home under the supervision of the eldest sister, whom Camilla had never met.

According to the surviving aunt and uncle, "Your father's eldest sister was not a safe person to be running the family. We later found out she was diagnosed as seriously unstable emotionally, but at the time all we knew is that she was big and strong and had a very short temper. When your father was six years old and he used to talk back to her, she always beat the crap out of him. The rest of us knew to stay clear of her anger, but your father tested her again and again. And each time she would get the better of him. It was horrible, and he kept it all inside. Your father has a lot of pride and he never wanted anyone to know about the beatings he took from his seventeen-year-old sister. He would be furious if he knew we were telling you about all this."

As Camilla looked at the photos of her father when he was seven, eight, nine, and ten, she saw his face looking more angry and withdrawn. The warmth and the lightness were gone from his expression and the eyes looked distant and sad.

Camilla realized from this research that her father was probably still secretly intimidated or resentful toward any woman who spoke up strongly like his eldest sister. Yet as a result of these family stories, Camilla discovered her freedom. She knew for the first time in her life that she wasn't going to wait any longer for her father to change into a suddenly warm and supportive mentor. Nor could she hold her breath hoping her father would become comfortable with the idea of a woman being strong and independent.

The next time she was at her family's house for a holiday meal, she looked with new eyes at her father. She no longer saw him as a bullying tyrant or a cruel person, but rather as a wounded individual who simply could not climb out of the protective shell he had put himself in long ago. She told me during a counseling session the week after her holiday meal with her family, "I sat looking at my father doing his 'I'm the boss' routine and I said a prayer of thanks that I now knew what was going on inside him. I said to God, 'Thank you for letting me see that my father's pain is not because of me but because of things that happened long before I came on the scene. Thank you for helping me find a way to love him again, even if he doesn't have the ability to verbalize his love for me.'"

Over the next several months, Camilla's business began to grow and she also found herself in a good relationship with a man who grew up with a single mom and has a lot of respect for strong women. During her final counseling session, Camilla told me, "I still have a father who says and does some stupidly sexist nonsense. But his comments no longer hurt me the way they once did because I know they're more about his pain than about my reality as a successful and healthy woman."

She continued, "Every once in a while when I'm visiting my family, I can sense that my father does secretly enjoy the fact that my business is doing well and that I'm in a good relationship. He can't say it out loud because that would blow his entire act, but I can see it in his eyes sometimes. There have been moments when I catch him looking in my direction and there's just the slightest glimpse of a smile on his worried and tense face. At those moments I know he loves me and I know that he respects me as much as he's ever been able to respect any woman. I'm lucky I hung in there to feel his love. It feels extremely good."

CHAPTER NINE

WHAT IF THERE'S BEEN SERIOUS PHYSICAL OR EMOTIONAL ABUSE?

I s there someone in your family who has crossed the line from being just unpleasant to being actually abusive? Is there a family member who sometimes engages in psychological abuse or emotional abuse, treating others in a cruel, vindictive, or highly manipulative way? Is there someone in your family who has been physically violent or sexually inappropriate in the past and in whose presence you still feel uncomfortable as a result? As you think about your own family, consider the following cases:

> Maura is a thirty-four-year-old fashion designer who has spent many years in therapy overcoming the psychological aftereffects of being molested by her father when she was ten years old. Fourteen months ago, Maura and her husband, Jay, had their first child and it stirred up a lot of confusion for Maura. "I see all the other moms getting relief, letting their kids spend time with loving grandparents,

but I don't know what to do about my own family situation. Should I even think about letting my parents help with my daughter or should I keep them out of her life altogether?"

Alec is a fifty-two-year-old widowed father of two grown children, one of whom is quite unstable emotionally. According to Alec, "I love my son, but he's quite violent and out of control at times. A few years ago at Thanksgiving he got angry about something and he smashed up several of my old photos and memorabilia. I haven't been willing to invite him to a holiday gathering since then, but I'm feeling a little guilty about it. How long do I need to put up a wall before I can reconnect with this troubled guy who still needs a lot of support?"

Recently a woman named Iris came up to me after a speech I gave at a holistic health center and she said, "I'm tired of hearing about ways to reconcile with difficult relatives. What if the family member is truly abusive? What if it's time to cut the ties with this toxic person?"

After hearing more about Iris's family situation, I thought about several of the counseling clients I have seen over the years who have extremely abusive relatives and who asked this same thing: When is it time to cut yourself off from a truly harmful person? This is an important question that needs to be addressed carefully. On the one hand, it would be tragic if any of us were to abandon or refuse to help family members who are seriously mentally ill, substantially memory-impaired, or chronically emotionally unstable. These relatives might be truly difficult, but they deserve our patience and our best efforts to help them without burning ourselves out.

For instance, there is a member of my wife's family who has been diagnosed with schizophrenia. At times he is a wonderful person to be with, and he has a rich knowledge of jazz, blues, electronics, and history. He understands the music of Miles Davis better than anyone I've met. Quite often he's humorous and loving. Yet at other times this relative says and does some very hurtful and harmful things. My wife Linda and I would never abandon him or stop doing what we can to help make his life better. We believe that being a part of a family includes taking care of those in the family who are unable to care for themselves.

On the other hand, there might be an abusive relative in your family who could get help to control his behavior and yet refuses to do so. In situations where the abusive person poses a physical threat to you or another family member, the only healthy choice may be to distance yourself from this individual and to stop letting her disrupt every family event. There are also situations in which you have to admit your own human limits and recognize that you might not be the right person to be the saintlike coach or relentless probation officer for an abusive relative who has absolutely resisted any help you've offered. Sometimes the only healthy choice is to let the outside world give this abusive individual the harsh consequences he seems to bring on.

But how do you know whether to hang in there or to get some distance from a harmful relative? How do you figure out when and how to protect the safety and sanity of the rest of the family? At some point it may come down to you establishing effective limits that say to the abusive family member, "If you want to participate in family events, there is a certain bottom-line decency that is necessary. If you're not willing to abide by these basic rules of respect, then we're going to need to care about each other from a safe distance."

In this chapter I provide you with specific questions and guidelines that can help you clarify the issues. How any limits get implemented, however, is up to you and your family members to work out together.

IS THERE A COVER-UP GOING ON IN YOUR FAMILY?

The first question for any family that has had to cope with someone's emotional cruelty, physical violence, or sexually inappropriate behavior is to ask, "Have we uncovered the full extent of the problem yet? Or are we still trying to downplay the situation or deny what really happened?"

Quite often when abuse has occurred or is occurring, people just don't want to face the full impact of what has been going on. It may be because family members are afraid or they are dependent on the very person who has been acting in an abusive way. If you try to get your relatives to address an abusive situation, especially one that has gone on for years, you might be accused of being too sensitive, hung up on the past, disloyal, or worse. Yet the longer the family "covers" for the offending relative and keeps the abuse a secret, the more confusion and pain is likely.

For instance, Nicholas, twenty-two, grew up with a hard-working but violent stepfather named Hal who often exploded in rages over the smallest incident. Nicholas has never been able to get his mother or his three older siblings to face what happened in their family. Nicholas explained, "My two brothers and my sister were a lot older than me; they weren't living at home when my parents got divorced and my mom started up with Hal. So they just don't want to deal with what happened to me, trapped with an explosive person who knocked out two of my teeth and left scars on the back of my legs and bruises on my ribs."

Nicholas continued, "My mother was there to witness much of it, but she's terrified of letting the truth come out because she doesn't want to lose Hal. Many times I would tell my brothers and my sister that Hal had whipped me with a belt or beaten me with a tennis racket. They'd say, 'Oh, don't exaggerate. Mom says it never happened.' The problem has always been that Hal can be quite generous and kind. He's helped each of my siblings with their college tuition and he's always buying things for my mom to keep her on his good side. Hal is quite the charmer when he wants to be. Yet at each family gathering I get sick to my stomach from trying to pretend we're one big happy family. My stepfather still gives me the creeps when he glares at me with that angry look of his. I've realized I'm not the kind of person who can just say 'Pass the eggnog' and pretend nothing happened all those years."

More than anything, Nicholas would like his mother and his other relatives to take him seriously and to stop covering for Hal. When Nicholas brought his mother and three siblings in for a family counseling session, it was difficult at first to get his relatives to stop downplaying what had happened between Nicholas and his stepfather. During the initial family session, Nicholas's older sister said, "Oh, for crying out loud. You're being too sensitive. This stuff, if it happened at all, took place a long time ago."

Nicholas responded, "But it's still happening. Just last month I got into a minor disagreement with Hal about how often I need to change the oil in my car. Hal shot me that look of his and he said, 'There you go being stubborn again. I ought to teach you a lesson.' I don't know what that means, 'teach you a lesson.' Is that an empty threat or is he going to do something vicious again? There's no way to be sure, and I don't feel much support from any of you about this."

For a moment it looked as though Nicholas was beginning to make some impact on his relatives. His eldest brother
commented, "I've seen that look in Hal's eyes. It's scary all
right, and maybe we need to back up Nicholas when he says
Hal is starting to threaten him again."

But Nicholas's mother quickly jumped in to downplay
each of the specific violent incidents that Nicholas claimed
Hal had been involved with. "Oh, you don't understand Hal,"
she insisted. "He's all bark and no bite."

Then Nicholas spoke up and said, "Wait a second. I
know I promised you, Mom, that I would never tell anyone
what I'm about to say, but I can't keep your secrets any
longer." Nicholas then informed his siblings that Hal had
broken two of their mother's ribs a few years earlier. There
was silence in the room for several seconds.

Nicholas's older sister asked the mother, "Mom, is it true
what Nicholas just said about Hal punching you during an argument and busting your ribs?" Nicholas's mother looked
down and said nothing. Then the sister repeated the question,
"Did it happen, Mom?"

"It only happened one time," the mother said.

The sister replied, "We've got to make sure it never happens again."

As a result of this chipping away of the family denial,
the family members were now ready to unify for the first
time and do something about the abusive situation that they
had been disregarding for twelve years. I suggested they

make a Family Protection Plan, which usually consists of three parts:

- First, what you will do *as a family* the next time your abusive relative says or does something inappropriate
- Second, how you will *warn* the abusive relative about what will happen if he or she does something threatening or harmful to anyone in the family
- Third, what you will *say* to the abusive relative to make it clear you care about this person but you will no longer tolerate the abusive behavior

When Nicholas and his siblings heard this description of a "Family Protection Plan," they began to brainstorm about how and when they would present their unified stance to Hal. Nicholas's mother seemed nervous about this sudden change in the status quo, but she kept silent as her four children joined together to make a plan to protect the family from future abuse.

After much discussion, this is the brief but powerful Family Protection Plan they developed:

1. If Hal said or did anything violent against Nicholas or anyone else in the family, the siblings were prepared to call the police and have him arrested.
2. This warning was going to be given to Hal by all of the siblings *together* in a family meeting the following week in my office.

3. The siblings were willing to say to Hal, "We know you love our mom and that she loves you. So if you successfully avoid making any threats of violence or any intimidating gestures toward Nicholas or the rest of us, then we'll do all we can to make sure you and Mom can continue to have a long-lasting relationship."

The next week there was another family meeting in my office, only this time with Hal in attendance. Nicholas and two of his siblings explained to Hal that they wanted future family events and holiday gatherings to be positive and comfortable for each member of the family. They told him calmly and respectfully that violence or threats of violence would not be tolerated.

I could see that Hal was a little surprised at how unified and firm the siblings had become. Hal said, "It looks like you guys have gotten your shit together. That's great. But I don't appreciate the insinuation that I'm a violent person or that you have anything to fear from me."

Then Hal paused and said, "But if you want to make a deal that we'll have no more threats and no more bossing each other around, I can live with that. You're grown up now and I'll do my best to treat you that way."

Nicholas's mom was quite nervous during the entire session and didn't say much until the end. That was when she finally spoke up and said, "Hal, I've never told you this because

I care about you so much and I didn't want to hurt you. But you need to know that all those years when you were being too rough with Nicholas, I was starting to think about ending our relationship. I hung in there and I'm glad I did. But please don't ever do anything to push me to make a choice between my children and my husband. I love each of you and I don't want to lose the closeness with any of you."

Then she looked at Nicholas for a moment and said, "I'm sorry I was weak at times, and didn't stand up for you when you needed me to. You deserved better and I hope someday you'll be able to forgive me."

Those were the words Nicholas had been waiting to hear for so many years. In Nicholas's case, he was fortunate that his siblings did unify with him to speak up and set limits toward the abusive family member. If Nicholas had not been able to get his older brothers and sister to join him in developing a Family Protection Plan, it might have been necessary for Nicholas to try one of two other options.

- First, he could have tried to enlist one or two family members who could back him up and be supportive allies even if his mother and some other relatives refused to take his side. In many families all it takes is for one or two family members to appreciate your point of view regarding an abusive relative and the situation begins to feel a little less overwhelming. Even if several family members continue to be charmed or swayed by the abusive relative, you can feel strong and sane from having solid allies on your side.

- Second, Nicholas could have chosen to reduce his exposure to Hal and show up only for holiday events and other visits when Hal was not in attendance. In families where the majority of family members refuse to face the truth about abusiveness that has gone on for years, the next best option is to choose which individuals and which events are safe and to keep some distance from events where the abusive relative is likely to dominate.

Even if the family holds it against you for keeping a healthy distance from the abusive individual, you have every right to take care of yourself. You can maintain your closeness with the healthy relatives in your family through phone calls, one-on-one visits, and written correspondence. You can "honor" your family by refusing to condone an unhealthy situation. In many cases, I have seen men and women maintain excellent relations year after year with one or more of their respectful relatives, even if they chose to avoid the big family events where the abusive relative tended to dominate. The goal is not to pretend you have a perfect family but to maximize whatever closeness you can achieve with your nonabusive relatives.

For example, I have a professional colleague named Gloria who grew up having to deal with an extremely violent and verbally abusive older brother. When she was younger, Gloria used to cringe in fear because her troubled older brother often destroyed her dolls and teddy bears in gruesome ways. As an adult, she has had several incidents in which her explosive older brother verbally attacked her and her children at family events. At a recent holiday dinner, the older brother got into a shoving match with Gloria's youngest son and it looked for a moment as if the incident might get violent, until Gloria's huge uncle stepped in to stop Gloria's older brother from going too far.

Gloria tried for years to get her parents and other siblings to face the truth about how much her older brother needs psychiatric treatment and firm limits. Yet the family refuses to deal with the problem and thinks Gloria is being "too sensitive." As a result, for the past two years Gloria has arranged satisfying one-on-one visits with the members of her family that she enjoys seeing. She has skipped the family gatherings where her brother might be in attendance. It's not a perfect situation, but it has allowed Gloria to enjoy warm moments with the family members she loves and to avoid being revictimized by the one family member who has threatened her. If this kind of situation sounds familiar to you, I recommend exploring with a counselor or friend what your options might be for maximizing your quality moments with family and reducing your exposure to an abusive relative.

IS THERE A WAY TO STOP THIS INDIVIDUAL FROM DOING MORE HARM?

In many families where there have been abusive incidents in the past, the possibility of limited contact with the offending relative is an ongoing possibility. For example, you might recall at the beginning of this chapter I mentioned Maura, a thirty-four-year-old fashion designer whose father molested her when she was younger and who now has to decide whether or not to let her young daughter get to know her grandparents. Should she let her parents be involved with her daughter or not?

During her counseling sessions, I asked Maura what her gut instinct was telling her to do. Maura explained, "There's a part of me that wants to say to my parents, 'You bloody idiots. You blew it. You crossed the line and there's no way I'm going to trust you ever again.' I can't trust my father because he's already proven he can at times be sneaky and selfish. And I can't trust my mother because for years she sided with him and tried to pretend I'd made the whole thing up."

Then Maura paused and said, "Yet there's also a part of me that remembers hundreds of fun moments growing up with my parents. My dad used to love to take us boating and hiking and windsurfing. My mom used to be so adorable when she'd sing to us or make us laugh with her silly faces."

Like many people who have survived physical and sexual abuse, Maura felt justifiably conflicted. On the one hand, her parents had betrayed her trust in a manner that should never be allowed to happen. On the other hand, they were the only parents she has ever known, and deep inside she still cares about them.

Maura told me, "I wish there were some way that my daughter could receive the love and doting that grandparents are supposed to give a young child. But how can I trust that they won't physically or subtly do something that might harm her the way I was harmed?"

At this point in her counseling, Maura was ready to explore some realistic options that might allow her daughter to experience the love of grandparents while at the same time protecting her daughter against any form of abuse.

One option is to make sure your abusive relative is never out of your sight when he or she is with a vulnerable child. Another option is to insist that your abusive relative enroll in a course or program for people who have crossed a harmful line. In some families that means your relative has to agree to take an extensive anger management course if he is going to be trusted to get control over his explosiveness or violence. In other families it means he has to agree to take a course or program in preventing child abuse or sexual abuse before he will be allowed to spend time with your child.

When I discussed these options with Maura, she said, "I would feel satisfied if my parents took a course on preventing child abuse and if I could guarantee that they're never alone with my daughter. That means my husband or I need to be

100 percent vigilant and fully present whenever my parents are around our daughter. Should they be allowed to babysit for us? No way! Should they be allowed to have private conversations that we can't see or hear? You've got to be kidding! Should I tolerate any strange comments or inappropriate tickling or touching? Not in a million years."

A few weeks later we held a session with Maura's parents in my office. Maura explained these supervision ground rules to her mother and father. At first her mother was a bit defensive, saying, "If you don't feel like you can trust us, then why do you even want us to be around the baby?" Maura replied, "Based on your history as parents, my first choice would be to say you can't visit my daughter. But I'm thinking about my daughter's best interests here. She deserves to have the love and affection of her grandparents—but only if the two of you are willing to abide by these rules."

Maura's parents looked at each other, and then the father said, "I think your suggestions are reasonable. I wish we could do more to help you out with babysitting because I know you've got a lot to handle right now. But if supervised visits and a course in child abuse prevention is what needs to happen, it's worth it. I understand that you have every reason to be careful after what happened when you were younger." Maura's mom nodded her head in agreement. "I just want to be able to have some time with my granddaughter. If supervision is what we need in order to make that possible, then that's what we need to do."

After the session I spoke with Maura on the phone. Neither Maura nor I was sure of whether her parents were telling the truth or saying what they thought we wanted to hear. When dealing with relatives who have proven themselves to be exceptionally self-centered or dishonest, it's often hard to tell when someone is being truthful or just manipulative. Despite her concerns, however, Maura told me, "I'm gonna take my daughter over next Sunday to visit with her grandparents. Wish me good luck."

In Maura's situation there was always some tension and distrust each time she or her husband watched her parents play or visit with their granddaughter. According to Maura, "I never was quite able to relax and say, 'Oh, isn't this sweet.' My mother and father might look to a naïve outsider like loving grandparents who can put a child's needs ahead of their own, but I know deep inside this is still somewhat risky. I expect to continue to monitor their visits closely as long as my daughter is young and vulnerable. I'd much rather be safe than sorry."

In your own family, is there an abusive relative who might be able to improve his or her behavior if watched closely? Or might there be some improvement if this person were to seriously engage in a course, program, or focused therapy to help overcome the attitudes and behaviors that made him or her so abusive in the past? Please note that I am in no way saying you should put yourself or your children at risk if you don't feel safe being around a relative who has proven already to be dangerous. Rather, the question is whether this dangerous person should be given another chance under very close supervision and very strict limits. Only you can make that choice.

IS IT TIME TO GET HELP IN DEALING WITH AN ABUSIVE FAMILY MEMBER?

Now we come to one of the toughest decisions that some families have to make. Even though we live in a society that says the family is a respected entity and we assume that each family should take care of its own members, nonetheless there are certain situations in which the family has to ask outsiders for help. If your abusive family member cannot stop being physically violent, sexually inappropriate, or interpersonally exploitative, there may come a time when you need to make the call to say, "Help! We can't resolve this on our own. We need people or resources that have more experience and better results with this kind of person."

For example, if you are the parent of a teenager or young adult who is posing a physical danger not only to your family but also to others in the community, it may be difficult but necessary to ask local agencies and experts for help in finding the right programs, facilities, and consequences to prevent your teen or young adult child from doing additional harm. Earlier in the chapter I mentioned Alec, whose young adult son had an anger problem. Alec found that his son was unwilling to accept any advice or counsel from him. Yet Alec's son did make some progress when Alec paid for him to attend a seven-week program on anger management run by a local nonprofit agency.

Knowing your limits and asking for outside help are crucial steps in resolving many other family dilemmas as well. If you are a sibling or spouse of someone with severe mood swings who sometimes crosses the line into verbal or physical abuse, you may need to start making phone calls to find the right health care professionals to assist your loved one. In many cases, the person can be helped with medication, psychotherapy, or support groups. The trick is finding the right professionals who can be both respectful and firm with your loved one.

Or if you are the adult child of a mentally impaired elderly parent who is posing a physical danger to others or to herself, you will need to start making calls to find out how to keep your troubled parent from doing harm. Or if you are in touch with a family member of any age whom you know is planning to do something destructive and this harm can be prevented, you have a responsibility to act.

In each of these cases, the challenge is to make sure you do the right thing and not to sit on your hands or wait for your worst fears to come true. I strongly recommend that if you suspect that your troubled family member is at all close to doing harm to anyone, including himself, you quickly start asking local agencies and counselors for information, options, and guidelines on how to take appropriate steps to prevent a tragedy from happening. Quite often close relatives are among the first to know that something isn't right with a loved one who is crossing the line into violence or harmful behaviors. It's your job to find out quickly how to keep your abusive relative from becoming or producing another crime statistic.

What's the Right Thing to Do?

Imagine for a moment that you were the sibling of Theodore Kaczynski, the isolated but brilliant man who was sending long, rambling notes and letter bombs to various university professors. If you were watching a television news report and you began to suspect that your brother might be the notorious Unabomber, what would you do? Would you hope your gut instinct was wrong or that the problem might go away if you ignore it? Would you try to help your troubled sibling elude capture? Or would you do what the actual sibling, David Kaczynski, did to prevent numerous deaths? He turned in his own brother to stop him from doing any more harm.

A less dramatic dilemma faced by many families is what to do if you suspect that a member of your family is bullying, neglecting, or verbally harming another family member. It might be a frustrated adult caregiver in your extended family who is starting to become abusive to an elderly relative who cannot adequately protect herself. Or it might be a short-tempered parent whom you suspect is being verbally abusive or physically cruel to a child whose behavior pushes this parent too far.

What is the right thing to do if you possess strong clues that there is child abuse or elder abuse occurring in your own family? In order to make this decision, there are three facts you need to keep in mind.

- First, it has been shown repeatedly that those individuals who are being abused feel betrayed not only by the abuser but also by the family members who remained silent or helped to cover up the abuse.

- Second, in most states it is a legal requirement that licensed health professionals can or must report suspected cases of child abuse or elder abuse—because otherwise the abuse tends to continue and get worse, while the perpetrator often moves on to harm other individuals as well.

- Third, no one that I've ever spoken with has ever said she felt comfortable or 100 percent certain when making a call to the appropriate agencies about child abuse or elder abuse. In fact, even when you have substantial proof that abuse or neglect is occurring, there will still be queasy feelings inside you, or a desire to close your eyes and pretend you don't know what you clearly do know.

I hope you never have to make such a painful choice, but if you suspect that your abusive relative is about to do something that could cause injury or death to innocent people, I urge you to do everything you can to keep your family member from bringing pain and suffering to other families.

"She's Got the Patience of a Floor Trader on Speed"

One of my counseling clients is Lucianne, a ceramic artist in her late fifties who recently told me about a painful decision she had to make. She had visited her elderly aunt Cloe, who suffers from Alzheimer's disease and is being cared for by Cloe's eldest daughter, Lucianne's cousin Eileen. During the visit, Lucianne witnessed several signs of neglect. Her mentally impaired aunt was sleeping in her own soiled underwear and had scratch marks and open sores on her arms and legs. Lucianne also overheard her cousin Eileen, a chronic drinker with a short fuse, screaming vicious remarks at Cloe, calling her a "witch," a "nightmare," a "monster," and an "idiot."

As Lucianne told me when she came in for counseling, "I was horrified to see how ugly the situation had gotten in only a few months since the last time I visited. I always knew my cousin Eileen was a bit intense. Her younger brother, who works for an investment banking company, said of Eileen, 'She's got the patience of a floor trader on speed.' But I had no idea she was crossing the line into mistreating her own mother."

I discussed with Lucianne two options for doing the right thing in a situation like this. I said, "We can call the police and they'll come over to investigate, but we won't know whether we've got a police officer who has experience with complicated eldercare situations or not. Or we can call one of the local agencies that specialize in this kind of dilemma; they'll help make sure Eileen doesn't continue to be left alone with her mom. And we can work with them to develop a healthier caregiving situation for Cloe and her family."

Over the next few days, several things happened. Lucianne called an elder protection agency that sent a caseworker to evaluate the situation. She also called several of Cloe's other relatives and arranged a family meeting with the caseworker. At the family meeting we came up with several options for improving Cloe's care, and for helping Eileen learn more effective ways of dealing with a relative who has Alzheimer's. Specifically, the caseworker and the family made the following Family Protection Plan:

1. Eileen was going to have to take a course in eldercare and be monitored by a caseworker before she would be allowed to be alone with Cloe again.

2. Eileen's younger brother, along with Lucianne and two other cousins, agreed to start paying what each could afford on a monthly basis to hire quality nursing care to help Cloe. They also agreed to start looking for a safe and clean nursing facility in the event that Cloe's home care became too costly or difficult.

3. Eileen's younger brother was given the assignment of handling some of the insurance and financial details

that had been especially stressful and frustrating for Eileen.

4. Lucianne agreed to make a few phone calls each week to remind aunts, uncles, cousins, and longtime friends that Cloe still needed visitors and that she still was able to appreciate many of the conversations and acts of kindness that these visitors brought to her.

What started out as a horrific abuse situation turned into a breakthrough for Cloe and her extended family. It didn't cure the Alzheimer's. Nor did it turn Eileen into Mother Teresa. Eileen continued to be somewhat edgy and impatient, but far less so than before she took the eldercare course and got support from the other relatives.

Yet it took Lucianne sticking her own neck out and making some difficult phone calls before the abusive situation began to improve. I urge you to make sure in your own family that you bring in knowledgeable outsiders for advice and assistance. Your job is not to fix overnight the long-standing personality clashes and abusive behaviors in your family, but if the situation calls for it you should be prepared to bring in people who can help—one step at a time.

CHAPTER TEN

HOW TO MAKE SURE FUTURE GENERATIONS WILL HAVE AN EASIER TIME

ow we enter the final chapter of this book. You may have thought when you first started reading chapter one that you were learning about how to deal with difficult relatives only in order *to help yourself*. But ten chapters later, you may have discovered that this topic of difficult family members is about much more than preventing your own indigestion or tension headache at the next holiday meal. This book has also been about preventing the kinds of mistreatment and miscommunication that damage our families and our world. It's about healing not only one's self but generations to come.

In this final chapter I will focus on four specific things you can do to increase the likelihood that your children, your grandchildren, your nieces, your nephews, and others will benefit from your insights and your positive steps toward improving things about your family situation. You will hopefully become one of the change agents that help make things better for those who will seek healthy closeness at your large and small family gatherings in the future.

What are the steps you can take starting right now to make your family atmosphere more nurturing and less upsetting for the next generation? Here are a few specific actions that have worked for many of my counseling clients.

ACTION #1: DO ALL YOU CAN TO BREAK AT LEAST ONE HARMFUL FAMILY PATTERN

In each chapter of this book we've explored a different irritating trait that one or more of your relatives may have brought to family interactions. Now comes the chance to choose at least one of these traits that you are committed to stopping or not repeating. For example, you might choose to refrain from criticizing family members about their weight, income, sex roles, or marital status, as certain of your relatives have. You might choose to be the first one who says to the members of the next generation, "It's fine to be who you are and not to twist yourself into a pretzel trying to meet the pressures this family has dished out at every gathering."

Maybe you will be the first member of your family to stop snapping angrily at the mistakes and imperfections of others and to start responding to your relatives with more compassion and sensitivity. Maybe you will be the first of your relatives to stop using sarcasm and condescension at family gatherings. Or maybe you will be the first member of your extended clan to appreciate and welcome into the family those outsiders who have been judged, gossiped about, and rejected for far too long. Or maybe you will be the first adult in your family to be a helpful mentor to one or two members of the next generation—instead of being wrapped up in your own self-interests and distractions.

Pruning the Family Tree

What is the one specific trait or behavior that you are interested in pruning from the family tree? Only *you* can decide. But imagine if each of the healthy members of your family did this as well. What would the future be like if they weren't saddled with the same harmful family patterns as you?

"Everyone in Our Family Has the 'Doing Too Much' Gene"

Here's a brief example of how making a commitment to being a change agent can help you focus on one family trait you want stopped. Mona is a forty-two-year-old counseling client of mine who works long hours as an art designer for television shows. According to Mona, "I grew up in a family where everyone was usually too busy with their own schedules to set aside much time to be together." Mona's father is a dedicated entrepreneur who still works seven days a week at his various businesses. Mona's mother is a schoolteacher and mystery book writer who usually is too busy to spend much quality time with her family. Mona's older sister is a medical researcher and university professor who hasn't taken a genuine day off or a nonworking vacation for several years. Mona's younger brother is a computer games designer whose company insists that working "part-time" means a sixty-hour week.

As Mona admitted, "It seems as if everyone in our family has the 'doing too much' gene. We're always saying we'd like to spend more time enjoying life or being with one another, but it never happens. And I'm realizing that my niece and nephew are growing up without my getting to spend very much time with them. It's sad because I don't have kids of my own and yet I'm always too busy to really connect with these two kids who are coming of age way too fast. I wish I could find the time to be a positive influence on them and maybe even to offer them some less-stressful options than their relatives and I have taken. But every week I'm under so many deadlines at work I just never get around to scheduling time with my niece or nephew. Pretty soon six months pass and they've changed beyond recognition again. It's so sad that all the adults in their life are too busy to truly connect with them."

During one of our counseling sessions I asked Mona, "How would you like to be the first member of your family to make a commitment to the next generation—to get beyond being 'too busy' and actually spend quality time with these kids who need a healthy sounding board about life and difficult choices?"

Mona's face lit up for a moment. "I would love to make

my niece and nephew a bigger priority than they've been." But then she thought for a moment and commented, "Except I am so swamped right now with work. How do I do this with my busy schedule?"

I told Mona what I have told many of my counseling clients who were unsure of how to find time for quality family moments. I said, "It starts with a commitment in your heart and then just a small amount of time firmly set aside from your daily and weekly schedule. I'm not talking about quitting your job or becoming a different person. I'm talking about making a conscious choice to be sure these kids remain an important part of your life."

In Mona's case, she began spending just one half hour a day on the phone talking with these two preteens and just a few hours each weekend committing to one-on-one time with her niece and nephew. As Mona described several months later, "It was the most rewarding choice I've ever made. Just a couple of hours each week taking my niece to museums and to her soccer games, or driving my nephew to his music lessons and basketball practice, has made a huge difference. We talk about all sorts of stuff in the car and when we stop for ice cream or dinner. Every few weeks I notice that something I've said or done has influenced the way they think or make choices."

Mona added, "Sometimes I talk with my niece and nephew about why there's so much pressure in our extended family to work so hard and be so results-oriented. These kids are right there with me with no bullshit, telling me exactly how it feels to them to be living with two workaholic parents and so many inflexible to-do lists. They love having someone they can open up with, someone who appreciates them unconditionally, and I'm very lucky to be able to give them the gift of being a family member who cares. I wish anyone in my family had been willing to hang out with me when I was younger and just talk to me like a person. It's the kind of family closeness I've always wanted but have never been able to achieve with any of my overstressed siblings, parents, aunts, or uncles."

ACTION #2: USE FILMS AND BOOKS TO HELP SORT OUT WHAT'S HEALTHY AND WHAT'S NOT

An extremely useful thing you can do to help future generations of your family make positive choices in life is to debrief them about the issues they will need to resolve in order to become sane adults. I have found as a therapist that films, books, magazine articles, songs, and short stories are often effective ways to spark conversations about the family issues that need addressing. These different means of expression become safe vehicles for talking about what's never previously been said.

For example, I once had a counseling client who grew up in a military family and wanted to sort out her mixed feelings about her uprooted childhood as a military brat. She had been raised by a passive, depressed mom and a strong but volatile dad who was a Marine sergeant. She was a fascinating person to counsel because at times she could be extremely strong and decisive like her dad, yet at other times she was withdrawn and frozen in fear like her mom.

To help generate ideas about how these two extreme personality traits stemmed from the realities of growing up in a military family, she and I each rented and watched the film *The Great Santini*. Based on a Pat Conroy novel, the film starred Robert Duvall as an explosive military officer home from war duty and Blythe Danner as his long-suffering wife. We also read portions of the book *Military Brats: Legacies of Childhood Inside the Fortress* by Mary Edwards Wertsch, about the many dilemmas and emotional issues faced by daughters and sons of career military personnel. Using these two resources to stir up feelings and identify crucial topics for discussion helped enormously. Instead of talking in generalities, we were hitting the core issues far more quickly and deeply. If you or some young relative you care about has grown up in a military family, these two gems can assist you in sorting out what has been churning inside for many years.

You may need to do some quick research to come up with the book, short story, or magazine article that touches on the specific issues that relate to your family. Then suggest a time to sit and eat popcorn with your younger relative while the two of you watch and discuss a rented video or DVD that portrays a resemblance to the family issues he or she faces. All you have to say is, "I would love to hear your reactions," and you'll be amazed at what these kids will tell you.

Finding the Right Resources

But where do you find the right films, books, articles, or stories to spark these healing conversations with your children, grandchildren, nieces, nephews, or other relatives? I recommend asking librarians, bookstore personnel, film rental store personnel, literature teachers, and others who can direct you to the proper resources. Or talk with a film expert, a well-read family member, a counselor, or a family advisor who can suggest age-appropriate creative works. Or look on the Internet, especially under the major bookstore sites like Amazon.com and Barnes and Noble, for their recommended books regarding a particular subject.

To give you just one idea, I recently asked a select group of prominent therapists and family experts for their top ten lists of the most dysfunctional families on film. Among the 120 therapists and family experts who responded, there was a wide range of selections. Here are a few of the "winners" that might be useful for your own multigenerational family conversations (with #1 receiving the most votes):

#10: *Divine Secrets of the Ya-Ya Sisterhood*—Based on two novels by Rebecca Wells, this is a good film to watch if you want to experience both revulsion and empathy toward a self-absorbed parent. It explores how the unfinished business of your parents' marriage can affect your own adult life and relationships.

#9: *Affliction*—Adapted from Russell Banks's novel, this Paul Schrader film with Nick Nolte and James Coburn is a painful look at how growing up with an abusive, alcoholic father can scar someone and alienate him from the people who care for him.

#8: *Where's Poppa?*—Based on a novel by Robert Klane, this zany 1970 comedy with George Segal and Ruth Gordon is about an elderly mother who is so controlling she goes to great lengths to disrupt her son's love life, even biting him on the butt in front of his new girlfriend.

#7: *Avalon*—This Barry Levinson film explores how an immigrant family of loyal siblings and cousins starts out unified but soon breaks apart because of family business squabbles, strong personalities, and holiday gatherings that are chaotic.

#6: *Punch-Drunk Love*—I didn't like this quirky Paul Thomas Anderson film starring Adam Sandler, but it sure provokes conversations about what it's like to be pressured by older sisters and to have a very short fuse.

#5: *American Beauty*—This is a disturbing look at a man who hates his suburban life and can't communicate

with his status-conscious spouse or his alienated, unhappy teenage daughter. Several experts called this
the most dysfunctional family ever filmed.

#4: *My Big Fat Greek Wedding*—You don't have to be
Greek to appreciate Nia Vardalos's comedic look at
how cultural differences, sexism, and a tradition-oriented father can affect a first-generation immigrant
family.

#3: *The Royal Tenenbaums*—A humorous look at how a
self-absorbed dad played by Gene Hackman and his
brilliant but unhappy kids can be so clueless about
how to handle adult commitments.

#2: *Terms of Endearment*—From Larry McMurtry's novel
about a mother and daughter who are so emotionally
intertwined it hurts.

#1: *Ordinary People*—Based on Judith Guest's novel and
directed by Robert Redford, this movie shows the
kind of lingering guilt, sadness, and rigidity that can
affect family members differently following the death
of a beloved child.

In addition to these well-known films, there were some
other choices from the survey and from my counseling experience that I'd like to pass along in the hope that they might
be useful. Several therapists and family experts recommended
rewatching *Cinderella* as a great way to stir up insights and

feelings about what it's like to be a neglected stepchild in a family where jealousy and competitiveness are prevalent. Several recommended *The Great Santini*, not just for its insights into military families but as the film most likely to stir up conversations in any family where a domineering father rules by intimidation or anger.

If there is someone in your family with a severe mental illness and the other siblings want a film that can help explore their own reactions to the ups and downs of living with such a troubled individual, I recommend *Dominick and Eugene*, which starred Ray Liotta and Thomas Hulce. If you have a family member who creates havoc because of his or her drug addiction, the other family members will probably benefit from watching and talking about the film *Ulee's Gold*; written and directed by Victor Nunez, it stars Peter Fonda as a beekeeper and devoted parent who raises his son's kids and somehow finds a way to maintain his dignity and stability despite painful family disruptions. If you would like a film that will spark conversations about adoption, sexual abuse by a sibling, or resilience despite a troubled childhood, I recommend the film *Antwone Fisher*, which was directed by costar Denzel Washington.

Finally, there is one other film that I have suggested to many of my counseling clients who were trying to help younger family members understand why holiday dinners and family gatherings are so stressful and conflict-prone. The film is called *What's Cooking?* and it came out in November 2000. It stars Alfre Woodard, Joan Chen, Mercedes Ruehl, and Kyra Sedgwick and it reveals how a Thanksgiving dinner brings out the best and the worst in four families—Jewish, Vietnamese, Latino, and African American—who live in the Fairfax District of Los Angeles. Prepare to laugh and cry, as you will see your own family stresses played out on the screen. No matter where your family comes from, you should have a lot to talk about.

ACTION #3: POINT OUT THE MEDICAL, FINANCIAL, AND PSYCHOLOGICAL CHALLENGES INHERENT IN YOUR FAMILY

You would be amazed at how many families never really talk about practical matters. The children and grandchildren are simply expected to figure it all out by themselves, and as a result they often feel confused or resentful about the challenges and opportunities that are quietly but surely passed down from their older relatives.

Airing Out the Family Closet

Every family has some skeletons in the closet that we wish the next generation wouldn't find out about. But the subconscious mind is forever trying to figure out what is hidden or unspoken. Quite often when someone comes into my office with a longtime compulsion or unhealthy pattern of financial, sexual, or psychological behavior—I would say in at least thirty percent of the cases—there is a family secret or hidden story that needs to be understood before the compulsion can be overcome. Furthermore, ailments such as late-onset diabetes, food allergies, and ulcers and other digestive disorders could be prevented or lessened if people talked about these risks early enough.

The following list suggests some helpful ways to clear the air and fill in younger relatives on family traits to watch out for:

- If your family has secrets, gives off mixed messages, or struggles with control issues regarding money and inheritances, is it possible that someone can talk about these taboo subjects sooner rather than later, so that younger relatives will have a better grasp of the financial challenges they will be facing?

- If your family is affluent, have you or anyone else ever talked honestly about some of the unfortunate side effects of having money, such as lack of motivation, focus, or perseverance, that can affect future heirs?

- If your family has relatives who've done jail time, been involved in feuds with various family members, had affairs that have been kept hush-hush, or who have children from other relationships, wouldn't you rather these stories came out in a calm conversation that you initiate at the right time than wait until a version gets shouted out in anger or bitterness at the most awkward moments?

- Has your family ever talked about which psychological issues should be watched for and responded to effectively because they tend to run in your family, such as depression, anxiety, panic attacks, bipolar disorder, or drug and alcohol dependencies?

- Has anyone in your family ever sat down and talked with the younger members of the family about why certain relatives don't get along or why a specific relative is so unpleasant some of the time and so loving at other times?

- Has there ever been a conscious effort made to explain to the next generations in age-appropriate ways the heroic and courageous things that some of their ancestors did under challenging circumstances?

- Have you ever made time to discuss with your younger relatives the strengths and difficulties of what it means to be a man or a woman in this family, or what it means to have the racial, ethnic, religious, or cultural issues that exist in your family?

- Do your relatives talk openly about your family's medical history and the risk of heart problems, high blood pressure, breast cancer, ovarian cancer, sickle cell anemia, Tay-Sachs disease, Huntington's disease, or any other illnesses that have shown up in your gene pool and should be watched for?

Most people love talking about trivia, while they may be extremely reluctant or ashamed to talk about real core issues that affect their family. What if instead of hiding the truth from the next generation you pointed out things they will need to know in order to cope better with life?

"I Wish Someone Had Just Told Me the Truth"
A few years ago I counseled Matthew, a man in his fifties who had spent much of his life making unfortunate choices in relationships. He told me during one of his counseling sessions, "For some reason I'm just not attracted to women who are down-to-earth and reliable. I always seem to be captivated by the women who are unpredictable, self-involved, and fiery."

As a result, Matthew had been married and divorced three times. Each time he found himself pursuing yet another unpredictable and unstable relationship. According to Matthew, "It's been quite costly because I care about each of these women and I continue to support them and the four kids who have resulted from these messy relationships. I would hate to make the same mistake again, but I still find myself drawn to women who my friends warn me are trouble."

During one of our counseling sessions, I asked him, "What were you told about your parents' marriage, and what does your gut tell you their marriage was like?"

Matthew described how his parents had been married for more than fifty-five years and claimed to have a successful marriage, even though Matthew has always wondered if there was something more they weren't telling him.

I asked Matthew, "What do you think they've never told you?"

"I don't know," he said.

So I asked Matthew to do some quick research and ask his living aunts and uncles what they knew about the early years of Matthew's parents' marriage. A few weeks later, Matthew came into my office and told me, "You're not gonna believe what I found out. According to one of my aunts, my mother was not always the cookie-baking and PTA mom I knew as a kid. When I was two years old, she supposedly had this passionate affair with her boss from the ad agency where she used to work. The guy promised he would divorce his wife and Mom was going to get a divorce as well so they could get married. But it never happened, and within a few years my mother had become the quiet and shut-down woman I experienced for all those years."

Matthew looked at me with an expression of relief and openness I had never seen in him before. He commented, "If someone had sat me down when I was eighteen years old and explained to me the complexities of who my mother is and what their marriage has been like, I feel as though this huge mystery would have been lifted off of me. I wish they had just told me the truth. I could've handled it and I believe I wouldn't have spent all these years on this quest to find the wild woman I was somehow going to rescue."

You may think you're doing the next generation a favor by glossing over such real stories about their relatives, but they want and need to understand. You may think it's ancient history or too private to discuss, yet I hope you will find the right time and place to bring these secrets to light. Only when your younger relatives have full access to the family history can they make sense of what happened long ago and how to change it for the future.

ACTION #4: WHY NOT BRAINSTORM WITH THE NEXT GENERATION TO RESOLVE FAMILY DILEMMAS?

In many families people are reluctant to talk with their children and grandchildren about family dilemmas. For example, if someone in the family has a chronic or acute illness, adults often try to hide this fact from the kids. The kids know something is going on, but instead of receiving the true story they get told half-truths and evasive remarks that make them feel suspicious or confused. Or, as another example, when there is a financial dilemma going on the kids might want to know why their parents are acting so tense. Instead, the adults bend over backwards trying to hide the truth, and so the kids surmise that something horrible is going to happen or that the adults are mad at them about something. Or the adults will pretend that money isn't a problem but then snap angrily at their kids for wanting to buy something.

Identifying the Elephant

Instead of trying to hide the elephant that everyone suspects is walking around in your family, sit down with your children, grandchildren, nieces, or nephews and say, "We need to have a family meeting about something important that is affecting all of us. We need your ideas and suggestions on how each of us can handle this situation better than we've been doing so far." The following example illustrates the value of including your younger family members in the loop when dealing with problems.

"We Didn't Think It Would Be Fair to Burden Them with This"

I recently counseled a married couple who were stressed out because the wife, Ingrid, had been diagnosed with multiple sclerosis and the husband, Bernard, was about to lose his job due to extensive layoffs in his industry. Despite the huge personal and financial pressures they were facing, Ingrid and Bernard had tried to pretend in front of their three kids that everything was fine. As Ingrid explained to me, "We didn't think it would be fair to burden them with this. We don't want our kids to worry."

Yet when the three children came in for a session, we

found out that the kids were well aware that mom and dad were acting strangely. The seventeen-year-old daughter, Aleesa, said, "Mom has been so short-tempered lately. I feel like whatever I do she finds fault with." The fourteen-year-old sister, Ginnie, commented, "My parents keep having these whispered conversations behind closed doors. All three of us kids are convinced they're about to get divorced." The youngest in the family, a ten-year-old son named Phillip, remarked, "I think what's going on is that Mom and Dad don't want to be parents anymore. They just seem way too busy with something else lately. I think they're gonna ask us to go live at our aunt's house, which would suck because it's four miles away and none of my friends are allowed to ride their bikes that far to visit me."

None of the three children knew exactly why things were so tense in their family, but they all sensed that something huge and dreadful was going on. As you will find in families that keep secrets, children will often imagine scenarios that are much worse than what is actually happening.

At the next counseling session with just Ingrid and Bernard, I asked, "Do you still feel you want to keep secret from your kids the facts about multiple sclerosis and the layoffs in your industry?" Ingrid was silent for a moment, and she looked at Bernard to see his reaction. Bernard put his hands up over his face and said quietly but firmly, "The children should *not* be told."

I waited for a few moments and then said, "I want to re-spect your wishes. But could you explain why you feel so strongly about this?"

Bernard remained silent as Ingrid said, "This is a huge issue for Bernard. When he was sixteen years old his father became seriously ill with Lou Gehrig's disease. All of a sudden, Bernard was no longer allowed to be an innocent child having fun or enjoying life. His parents insisted he get a job and help support the family. He also had to help his mother raise the three younger siblings. And he had to watch his strong and independent father rapidly decline and become physically dependent from this terrible illness."

Bernard continued to sit in silence and Ingrid added, "I feel as though my husband has carried a huge load of resent-ment and pain inside him ever since his family situation forced him to grow up so suddenly. That's why he is so moody and difficult to reach at times. And that's why I'm afraid my being diagnosed with MS is going to cause him to feel overwhelmed and resentful."

During the rest of that counseling session, I explored with Bernard what it had been like as a sixteen-year-old having to suddenly carry so much of the load for his family. I wouldn't say that Bernard was exactly talkative, but he did re-veal to Ingrid and me his greatest fear: "That my own three kids would lose their childhood and always resent us for it."

As with most psychological issues, there was some truth to Bernard's concerns, but there were also some inaccurate perceptions. I said to Ingrid and Bernard, "I agree with you that it would be unfair and harmful if you suddenly demanded of your kids that they rush in and try to save the family from the physical illness and the financial stresses that are beyond what any child can handle. I completely understand that you don't want to force your kids to surrender their innocence and their childhoods because of these huge new challenges in your family."

Yet I also suggested, "There's another way of looking at this situation. If you sit down with your children and treat them respectfully as smart and caring individuals, you can ask for their ideas and suggestions on what they would feel good doing to help out and what they think would be unfair or excessive. If you reassure your kids that you value their intelligence and that their opinions are important, you might be surprised at how they will come up with some options that successfully balance the need to help out the family and the need to still have a nonpressured childhood."

At first, Bernard was skeptical. "Do you really think these kids are old enough to be able to understand what's going on right now in our family?"

I replied, "I don't know for sure. They're your kids and you know them a lot better than I do. But my experience has been that if you ask a seventeen-year-old, a fourteen-year-old, and a ten-year-old for suggestions on how to help out during a family crisis while at the same time making sure they still have their normal routines and pleasures as kids, you will be amazed at how many good and practical ideas they'll come up with."

Ingrid looked at her husband and said, "Bernard, trust me on this. Of course I want them to get to be kids, but I really believe this could be a chance for our children to feel we respect them and their contributions to the family."

Bernard thought without speaking for almost a minute, and then he finally replied. "I'm not so convinced, but I'll give it a try."

So at the next counseling session, I invited the entire family to start working together and brainstorming about what each of them could do to make things easier in light of the medical and financial stresses they were facing—and to make sure there was still time and energy for doing the things each of these kids enjoyed doing most. This was the beginning of a huge change in how this family operated. For the first time the kids were being given a crucial role in problem solving and family teamwork. For the next hour, each family member came up with several good ideas on how they could stay balanced while also pitching in to help respond sensibly to the current crisis.

The middle child, Ginnie, offered to cook meals and let her mom rest more, but she also explained that she wouldn't be able to cook on Tuesday or Thursday nights when she has her gymnastics classes. The eldest daughter, Aleesa, said she was willing to take on a part-time job as a bookkeeper for her aunt's entertainment management firm to help her parents stay afloat financially, but that she still wanted to reserve Friday and Saturday nights for going out with her boyfriend. The youngest child, Phillip, offered to take out the garbage each week, clean up the kitchen once a day, and do his homework each night without his parents having to beg him; but he added, "I still want to be able to watch my favorite shows on television for one hour each day and three hours on weekend mornings," to which Ingrid replied, "Two hours maximum television on weekends." Phillip smiled as he said, "I thought I could get one past you, Mom, but you're still pretty sharp."

As part of the family brainstorming, Ingrid offered to join a weekly MS information group so that she could keep up with the best strategies for managing her illness. She also told her children, "I want to make sure I'm still involved in your daily homework and your everyday decisions. Don't think that just because I'm ailing there's no one here watching you." Bernard promised to spend at least three hours each day looking for a new job and one hour each day working out at the gym to make sure he didn't slip into depression.

Rather than being a shameful burden, the family stresses became an opportunity for these five individuals to rally together. It became a chance for the next generation to learn about teamwork, balance, good communication, and mutual respect.

I have found in numerous families that once the members stop hiding from the truth and instead call upon each individual to brainstorm on what can be done, it almost always strengthens the family. These family brainstorm meetings can be especially effective if you make it clear from the start that you want each family member to stay balanced and avoid burning out—to do a lot to help the family but also to reserve time and energy for his or her individual needs and pursuits.

As Ingrid said a few months after this brainstorming session, "I'm sorry it took MS and layoffs in my husband's industry to get my family feeling closer and more loving than ever. But these past few months have been an unexpected blessing because I see all three of my kids developing parts of their personalities they never had to tap into before. It's been a frightening time for our family, and yet I'm seeing that each of my kids is growing up with a good feel for how to honor his or her own needs while at the same time helping others. That's something I wish I'd learned as a kid."

LOOKING FOR PROGRESS, NOT PERFECTION

As with many of the cases in this book, I hope you recognize in the above example that when it comes to family dilemmas there are rarely perfect solutions or painless options. In most family situations there will always be some complicating factors and some difficult relatives to keep things interesting. The family meeting didn't cure Ingrid's multiple sclerosis, but it did allow her to feel the strong family support that's necessary for her ongoing care. The brainstorming session didn't suddenly turn Bernard into an outgoing, fun-loving individual, yet it did help him see that his children were turning out a lot healthier and more balanced than he had thought they would, in spite of his job situation.

I cannot promise you that after reading this book your family stresses will disappear. Instead, I predict that your narcissistic relatives will still be somewhat self-absorbed and your impulsive relatives will still be impulsive. But isn't that the beauty of being part of a family? Even with all the conflicts and disagreements, there can be a profound level of caring and commitment.

Yes, there will still be moments when you look around at a family gathering and you say to yourself, "My goodness, am I strong enough to survive these people?" There will still be moments when you mutter under your breath, "Why does this particular person have to be so difficult year after year after year?"

I wish for you and your loved ones continued strength and courage as you address the ups and downs that take place in your immediate and extended family. I hope you have many moments of closeness and celebration with the relatives you enjoy as well as fewer moments in which your most difficult relatives get on your nerves. Please don't forget that dealing with family issues is a lifelong process of learning and discovery. Yet it's definitely worth the effort, because future generations will be better off because of each step you take to improve the level of respect and compassion among your relatives.

Remember, the goal is not to have a perfect family but rather a sense that with each passing year you are making some progress in how you connect with these complex people who are a crucial part of your journey in life.

APPENDIX:

ABOUT THE
RESEARCH STUDY

For more than twenty years I've been conducting workshops at UCLA Extension and other adult education programs for men and women of all ages regarding their difficult relatives. At these events I often get asked, "What percentage of people have difficult relatives and family conflicts?"

Usually the person asking the question admits that he or she feels somewhat alone in having family clashes or expects he or she is part of a small percentage of people who have serious family stresses year after year. I've noticed that most individuals assume the majority of families are well behaved or harmonious; most people are concerned or embarrassed that their particular family has a number of feuds, tensions, or personality clashes.

I knew I couldn't answer the question "What percentage of people have difficult relatives and family conflicts?" just based on my clinical psychotherapy practice or the unrepresentative sample of individuals who sign up for workshops about family dilemmas. So several years ago I began looking to see if there were any scientific studies or polling research that might address this issue.

I never could find a statistically valid scientific study or poll that might answer this question of what percentage of people have easy relatives and what percentage have difficult relatives. I decided to conduct a carefully designed research study of over 1,400 randomly selected men and women to find out just how rare or common these family tensions tend to be. My hope was to interview a realistic and statistically valid nationwide sample across all races, ethnicities, ages, income groups, and family backgrounds that would give us a good estimate of just what goes on behind closed doors in our immediate and extended families.

The design. A statistically significant research sample of over 1,400 people were randomly selected from the phone books of large and small communities in eleven of the fifty United States and asked the following questions:

1. Do you have just 2 minutes for a quick survey? All answers will be kept private and confidential.

2. Do you have any immediate or extended family who get together for holiday meals, birthday meals, or other family events?

3. How would you describe your family holiday events and get-togethers?

   a. Enjoyable

   b. Sometimes enjoyable, but sometimes very difficult

   c. Rarely enjoyable, but an obligation I do anyway

    d. We don't get together because of (death, geography, tensions, no one initiates)

4. Is there someone in your immediate or extended family who gets on your nerves?

5. Have you ever dreaded going to a family holiday event because of a personality clash with one of your relatives?

6. What have you enjoyed about family holiday get-togethers?

The results. Over 92 percent (1,358) of the random individuals who were reached did answer the survey. Less than 8 percent said they were too busy, or they refused to answer the survey after being asked only the first question, "Do you have just 2 minutes for a quick survey?"

Here are the actual numbers and percentages for the rest of the questions and answers:

2. Do you have any immediate or extended family who get together for holiday meals, birthday meals, or other family events?

    76 percent (1,041) said yes, 23 percent (317) said no

3. How would you describe your family holiday events and get-togethers?

    a. Enjoyable—32 percent (332)

    b. Sometimes enjoyable, but sometimes very difficult—41 percent (427)

    c. Rarely enjoyable, but an obligation I do anyway—27 percent (282)

    d. We don't get together because of (ranked according to frequency of response): geography, death, tensions, no one takes the initiative

4. Is there someone in your immediate or extended family who gets on your nerves?

Yes—77 percent (913); no—23 percent (445)

5. Have you ever dreaded going to a family holiday event because of a personality clash with one of your relatives?

Yes—58 percent (788); no—42 percent (570)

6. What have you enjoyed about family holiday get-togethers?

There was a range of answers, including many who said "To catch up with family members I miss and love," "To see the younger ones," "To spend time with loved ones who are getting older," "The food," "The traditions," "The camaraderie," "The laughter," "The sense that we all have something in common," etc.

Please note that there is a statistical margin of error of (plus or minus) 3 percentage points for each of the questions and answers described above.

Conclusions. What does this research mean to you and your family situation? Here are some conclusions that can be drawn from the study:

1. The initial hypothesis or assumption of most people is wrong. It turns out that if you have family conflicts or difficult relatives, you are neither alone nor part of a small percentage of troubled families. In fact, this study reveals for the first time the widespread prevalence of family personality clashes, which are much more prevalent than my colleagues or I expected. Over 75 percent of Americans have a relative who gets on our nerves. More than 67 percent of us find our family get-togethers to be "sometimes very difficult" or "an obligation that is rarely enjoyable, but I do it anyway."

2. A large number of families have ambivalent feelings each year when religious or secular holidays roll around. This study reveals that only 23 percent of families avoid each other altogether while the vast majority of families get together even though they find the events "difficult at times" or they are at odds with at least one family member.

3. Most of the respondents, including most of those who said they have difficult relatives or stressful family get-togethers, still had some good things to say about their family gatherings. It seems that even if there are difficult moments, there is still a strong desire to connect with family members at various times during the year.

4. Rather than feeling ashamed or deficient for having a difficult family situation, it seems more accurate according to this study to see yourself as part of the vast majority of men and women who desire family connection but who have to contend with one or more difficult relatives each year.

Future research. I hope there will be additional studies in the future to clarify or refine any or all of these conclusions. Research that helps us understand what goes on in our families and how to respond more effectively to our difficult relatives is long overdue.

SOURCES AND
SUGGESTED READINGS

Chapter One, page 6

"In the past ten years there have been some exciting discoveries by the scientists conducting the human genome project. . . . One of the remarkable findings has been that there seems to be, *by design*, a range and severity of personality diversity among members of the same family."

This research is summarized in the book *Shadow Syndromes* by John Ratey and Catherine Johnson (New York: Pantheon, 1997) in "New Brain Science: Is Everybody Crazy?" by Sharon Begley, *Newsweek* magazine, January 26, 1998, pages 50–56, and in "The Blank Slate: Why Are We Who We Are?" *Discovery* magazine, October 2002, pages 34–40.

Chapter One, page 7

"Genetic research shows that in families there are usually one or two people who are prone to narcissistic tendencies. . . ."

The three sources listed above (*Shadow Syndromes*, *Newsweek* 1/26/98, and *Discovery* 10/02) describe the genetics research on personality disorders. For more on the specific issue of narcissistic family members, see *The Diagnostic and Statistic Manual of Mental Disorders*, Fourth Edition (Washington, D.C.: The American Psychiatric Association, 1994), pages 658–661; *Children of the Self-Absorbed* by Nina Brown (Oakland, Calif.: New Harbinger, 2001); *The Narcissistic Family* by Stephanie Donaldson-Pressman and Robert Pressman (San Francisco: Jossey-Bass, 1997); and *Why Is It Always about You?* by Sandy Hotchkiss (New York: Free Press, 2002).

Chapter One, page 9

"As Reinhold Niebuhr said so eloquently almost eighty years ago . . ."

He first said the Serenity prayer in his sermons to his congregation and it can be found in *The Essential Reinhold Niebuhr* by Robert McAfee Brown (New York: Yale, 1987).

Chapter Two, page 27

"But scientific studies have taught us since that unloading on someone doesn't actually reduce the level of anger . . ."

For insights into why venting anger doesn't help either the person doing the venting, the person receiving the venting, or the relationship between the two people, see *Anger, the Misunderstood Emotion* by Carol Tavris (New York: Simon and Schuster, 1989); "The Expression of Anger and Its

Consequences," by Jerry Deffenbacher, in *Behavior Research and Therapy*, Volume 34, 1996b, pages 575–590; and *Treatment of Patients with Anger-Control Problems and Aggressive Behaviors* by Donald Meichenbaum (Waterloo, Ontario: University of Waterloo, 2001).

Chapter Two, page 29

" . . . in the 1983 film *The Big Chill* . . ."

Was written by Lawrence Kasdan and Barbara Benedek, Columbia/TriStar Pictures.

Chapter Two, page 49

" . . . Arnold Beisser developed and studied the effectiveness of something he called *the paradoxical theory of change*. . . ."

This 1970 article can be found on pages 77–80 of an anthology titled *Gestalt Therapy Now* by Joen Fagan and Irma Shepherd (New York: Harper, 1970).

Chapter Three, page 84

" . . . the *Challenger* space shuttle . . ."

For more on the scientific explanations of what happened, see "Challenger Disaster," *Microsoft Encarta Online Encyclopedia 2002*.

Chapter Four, page 96

" . . . the National Conference of Community and Justice . . ."

can be reached by contacting your local NCCJ office (see the

Web site www.nccj.org for addresses and phone numbers) or
contact the national office at 475 Park Avenue South, 19th
Floor, New York, NY 10016, (212) 545-1300.

Chapter Four, page 112

"Is there a book, an ongoing activity, or a one-time event that
you would be willing to experience with an open heart . . ."

In addition to whatever you and your family member
choose for the other person to experience and understand
about your different spiritual paths, there is also an excellent
series of books written for people who want to be respectful
and compassionate toward the religious and spiritual practices
of others. The books are titled *How to Be a Perfect Stranger: A
Guide to Etiquette in Other People's Religious Ceremonies*, by
Stuart Matlins and Arthur Magida (Woodstock, Vt.: SkyLight
Paths, 1999).

Chapter Five, page 134

"In my earlier book *The Ten Challenges* . . ." refers to *The Ten
Challenges: Spiritual Lessons from the Ten Commandments for
Creating Meaning, Growth and Richness Every Day of Your
Life*, by Leonard Felder (New York: Harmony/Crown, 1997),
page 130.

Chapter Seven, page 175

". . . a black-and-white version of the classic film *Dr. Jekyll
and Mr. Hyde* . . ." refers to the 1932 Oscar-winning film with

Frederic March, directed by Rouben Mamoulian, from the story by Robert Louis Stevenson.

Chapter Seven, page 176

"According to the most recent statistics . . ."

The numbers of men and women who abuse alcohol or drugs come from the Web site www.well.com from data compiled by the U.S. Department of Health and Human Services, Office for Substance Abuse Prevention. The statistics on prescription drug abuse are from "Abuse and Misuse of Medications," by Thomas Patterson, Jonathan Lacro, and Dilip Jeste, in *Psychiatric Times*, Volume XVI, Issue 4, April 1999.

Chapter Eight, page 219

" . . . a series of religious position papers, articles, and speeches put together by Rabbi Elliott Dorff . . ."

For more on the debate within Conservative Judaism about gay and lesbian equality, see "Out of the Closet: Will the Conservative Movement Reopen the Issue of Gay Rabbis?" by Julie Gruenbaum Fax, *The Jewish Journal of Greater Los Angeles*, Volume 17, Number 47, January 17–23, 2003, pages 12–13; and *Love Your Neighbor and Yourself: A Jewish Approach to Modern Personal Ethics*, by Elliott Dorff (Philadelphia: Jewish Publication Society, 2003).

Chapter Eight, page 223

The Biblical passage "And the truth shall set you free" is from John 8:32.

Chapter Eight, page 225

"Parents and Friends of Lesbians and Gays (PFLAG)" refers to a national support organization with open meetings in most cities for family members and friends who want to understand their loved ones and their own discomforts and fears. It can be reached by looking in your local phone book, or you can find local meetings at www.pflag.org, or by contacting the national office at 1726 M Street NW, Suite 400, Washington, DC 20036, (202) 467-8180.

Chapter Eight, page 226

" . . . three different written viewpoints on the issue . . . "

I urge you to ask for various viewpoints from your own minister, priest, or rabbi to find out about debates and differing views within your particular denomination. In addition, you can find various viewpoints on religion and homosexuality in *What the Bible Really Says about Homosexuality*, by Daniel A. Helminiak (a Roman Catholic priest) (San Francisco: Alamo Square Press, 2000); *Openly Gay, Openly Christian*, by Samuel Kader (a Protestant minister) (San Francisco: Leyland Publications, 1999); *Welcoming but Not Affirming*, by Stanley J. Grenz (an Evangelical minister) (Louisville: Westminster John Knox Press, 1998); and *Lesbian Rabbis: The First*

Generation, by Rebecca T. Alpert, Sue Levi Elwell, and Shirley Idelson (a Reconstructionist rabbi and two Reform rabbis) (Piscataway, N.J.: Rutgers University Press, 2001).

Chapter Ten, page 267

" . . . the book *Military Brats* . . ." refers to *Military Brats: Legacies of Childhood inside the Fortress,* by Mary Edwards Wertsch (Bayside, N.Y.: Aletheia, 1996).